The New Grammar in Action 1

Barbara H. Foley

with Elizabeth R. Neblett

Union County College
Cranford, New Jersey

HEINLE
CENGAGE Learning

Australia • Brazil • Japan • Korea • Mexico • Singapore • Spain • United Kingdom • United States

HEINLE
CENGAGE Learning

The New Grammar in Action 1
Barbara H. Foley with Elizabeth R. Neblett

Managing Developmental Editor: Amy Lawler
Production Services Coordinator: Maryellen E. Killeen
Market Development Directors: Jonathan Boggs and Thomas Dare

Also participating in the publication of the program were:

Vice President and Publisher, ESL: Stanley Galek
Associate Developmental Editor: Joyce La Tulippe
Director of Global ELT Training: Evelyn Nelson
Manufacturing Coordinator: Mary Beth Hennebury
Project Manager: Hockett Editorial Service
Photo/Video Specialist: Jonathan Stark
Interior Designer/Compositor: Greta D. Sibley & Associates
Cover Designer: Gina Petti/Rotunda Design House
Illustrator: James Edwards
Photo Researcher: Katherine Hughs

ISBN-13 978-0-8384-6719-0
ISBN-10 0-8384-6719-9

Heinle
25 Thomson Place
Boston, MA 02210
USA

Cengage Learning is a leading provider of customized learning solutions with office locations around the globe, including Singapore, the United Kingdom, Australia, Mexico, Brazil and Japan. Locate our local office at:
international.cengage.com/region

Cengage Learning products are represented in Canada by Nelson Education, Ltd.

Visit Heinle online at **elt.heinle.com**
Visit our corporate website at **cengage.com**

Photo Credits All photos by Jonathan Stark except where noted: photos by Elizabeth Neblett pp. 2 top right, 6, 9, 20, 36, 39, 44, 53, 72, 142, 148, 149; photos by Stock Boston pp. 67 top right, middle left, 116 top left, 150 top right, 168; , photo by Bogard Studio p. 151 bottom; photo by Sygma Photo News p. 155

ACKNOWLEDGMENTS We wish to thank the faculty and students at the Institute for Intensive English, Union County College, New Jersey, for their support and encouragement during this project. Many faculty members previewed the units in their classrooms, offering suggestions for changes and additions. Students shared stories and compositions, and smiled and posed for numerous photographs. Thanks, also, to the staff at Heinle & Heinle, who remained encouraging and calm throughout the development and production of this revision.

Printed in the United States of America
24 20 19 18 17

Contents

To the Teacher

The New Grammar in Action, a three-level grammar series for secondary and adult ESL/EFL students, offers a dynamic, communicative approach to language learning. The series presents English language structure and practice through inviting contexts such as family, jobs, downtown, growing up, weather and vacations. Bold, lively illustrations, authentic student photographs, and information-rich charts and graphs illustrate each context for practice and use of each structural focus. The series offers a wealth of variety for students and teachers to engage in both whole class and small-group activities. Listening components to each unit guide students to identify structures in context and in use, progressing from controlled presentation to more open-ended, interactive language use. Throughout the text, students are encouraged to share their ideas and experiences, to think more critically about subject matter, comparing and contrasting ideas as they gain greater control and confidence in the target language.

GRAMMAR IN ACTION

Grammar in Action sections introduce each unit, setting the context and grammar focus. Listening activities are accompanied by illustrations to assist students in comprehending a new topic and related vocabulary. Before listening to the tape, students may be asked to practice new words and forms, describe a picture and make predictions about what they are about to hear. Students may ask to hear the listening as many times as they wish. Listening sections are structured to allow students the opportunity to follow pictures in sequence, identify words and phrases, fill in information, and comprehend natural language forms in use.

Activities in the **Grammar in Action** section are varied for whole class and pair oriented work, appealing to diverse learning styles while directing students to answer questions, complete sentences, provide information about themselves, form sentences from cues, give directions and describe illustrations. In this way, *Grammar in Action* units set the tone for high student interest and interaction during classroom time.

WORKING TOGETHER

Working Together sections give students the opportunity to work with a partner or a small group on more open-ended, communicative exercises presented within the context of the unit. Grammar is put into immediate use in the form of interviews, surveys, role plays, chart and graph skills as well as problem-solving activities. Students are encouraged towards fluency with the exchange of ideas.

Information gap exercises, identified as **Student to Student** sections, are included throughout most of the **Working Together** units. These sections allow for both controlled and open-ended practice between students. Students work in pairs, each looking at a different page. Students share and exchange ideas though challenging exercise that ask them to find information, to fill out charts and graphs, recognize differences, match questions and answers, and think about a topic in new ways.

PRACTICING ON YOUR OWN

Practicing on Your Own sections allow students the time to internalize the structures presented within each unit through written practice and expression. This section is useful for individual homework and review. Students gain more confidence writing and thinking in the target language as they compete cloze exercises, sentence completions, and question formations typically found within standardized language tests. As these units continue, students progress to more exercises that ask them to contrast structures and forms of language.

SHARING OUR STORIES

Most units include **Sharing Our Stories** sections with authentic essays and narratives by and about ESL students and their experiences. These personal narratives are points of departure to stimulate student story-telling and writing. After reading these stories, students are encouraged to write about their own lives and experiences. Additionally, there are other opportunities presented throughout the text, marked by a writing icon, for students to expand on a topic or idea through their own personal written expression.

HAVING FUN WITH THE LANGUAGE

The Having Fun with the Language section outlines expansion activities for both in and outside of class time. Suggestions for surveys, games, interviews and research and library work give students the chance to play with language in new contexts. These units are especially helpful for students who may be wrestling with a troublesome skill or structure, as students and teachers alike can select activities of high interest and appeal.

GRAMMAR SUMMARY

These sections offer additional structural focus throughout each unit by providing an overview of the grammar for the lesson. Explanations are brief and clear, appropriate for beginning and high-beginning students. Appendices at the back of the book offer additional support and reference material.

Teachers will view *The New Grammar in Action* as both a solid basis for classroom instruction and a text which allows for creative expansion of grammar structures in form and use. Over time, teachers will personalize their use of the series, expanding the units with current magazine articles, charts from newspapers, workshop ideas, and more.

Personal Information

Present Tense of *Be*

◣ A. INTRODUCE YOURSELF *Introduce yourself to another student or to the class.*

My name is _____ . I'm from _____ .

I am _____ years old.

I live in _____ .

I'm married.   *or*   I'm single.   *or*   I'm divorced.

I have _____ children.   *or*   I don't have any children.

I'm at school now. I'm in Room _____ .

B. LISTEN: PERSONAL INFORMATION
*Listen to the information about each picture. Write **Yes** or **No** on the line before each statement.*

1.

1. __Yes__ Ana is from Mexico.

2. _____ She's 19 years old.

3. _____ She's a student.

2.

4. _____ Kashif is from Pakistan.

5. _____ He's single.

6. _____ He's at school now.

3.

7. _____ Kim and Su-Jin are married.

8. _____ They're single.

9. _____ They have one child.

4.

10. _____ Texas is a state.

11. _____ The capital is Austin.

12. _____ Texas is small.

2

■ C. PRONOUNS *Say the sentence again with **he, she, it** or **they.***

> **EXAMPLE**
>
> Ana is at school.   **She** is at school.

1. Ana is from Mexico.
2. Kashif is from Pakistan.
3. Kim and Su-Jin are from Korea.
4. Ana is single.
5. Kashif is at work.
6. Kim and Su-Jin are married.
7. Texas is big.
8. The students are at school.
9. The teacher is in the classroom.
10. The book is on the desk.
11. The books are on the table.
12. The students are from India.
13. The door is open.
14. The teacher is at work.

■ D. CONTRACTIONS *Say the sentence again with a contraction.*

> **EXAMPLE**
>
> **We are** students.   **We're** students.
>
> He **is not** from Cuba.   He **isn't** from Cuba.

I am	→	I'm
he is	→	he's
she is	→	she's
they are	→	they're
we are	→	we're
is not	→	isn't
are not	→	aren't

1. We are at school.
2. You are in the classroom.
3. They are in Room 5.
4. They are not in Room 8.
5. I am not married.
6. I am single.
7. He is not at work.
8. He is at school.
9. She is from Mexico
10. It is the capital.

■ E. ASK AND ANSWER *Ask and answer these questions about the pictures.*

> **EXAMPLE**
>
> **Are you single?**   **Is Kashif single?**   **Is Ana single?**   **Are they married?**
>
> Yes, I am.   Yes, he is.   Yes, she is.   Yes, they are.
>
> No, I'm not.   No, he isn't.   No, she isn't.   No, they aren't.

1. Is Ana Luisa from Japan?
2. Is she single?
3. Is she at home?
4. Is Kashif a student?
5. Is he at home now?
6. Are Kim and Su-Jin married?
7. Are they from Russia?
8. Are they at school now?
9. Is Texas a big state?
10. Is Austin the capital of Texas?

A. INTERVIEW *Sit in a group of three students. Complete the information in the first form about yourself. Then ask questions and complete this information about your partners.*

REGISTRATION FORM

NAME: _____

ADDRESS: _____

CITY: _____

ZIP CODE: _____

TELEPHONE NUMBER: _____

BIRTHDATE: _____

LANGUAGE: _____

What's your name?

What's your address?

What's your zip code?

What's your telephone number?

What's your birthdate?

What language do you speak?

REGISTRATION FORM

NAME: _____

ADDRESS: _____

CITY: _____

ZIP CODE: _____

TELEPHONE NUMBER: _____

BIRTHDATE: _____

LANGUAGE: _____

REGISTRATION FORM

NAME: _____

ADDRESS: _____

CITY: _____

ZIP CODE: _____

TELEPHONE NUMBER: _____

BIRTHDATE: _____

LANGUAGE: _____

◼ B. FIND SOMEONE WHO *Walk around the classroom and ask these questions. For each question, write the name of a classmate who says,* **Yes, I am.** *For each question, write the name of a classmate who says,* **No, I'm not.**

Question	Yes, I am.	No, I'm not.
Are you from Mexico?		Boris
Are you eighteen years old?		
Are you married?		
Are you single?		
Are you a student?		
Are you a teacher?		

Write five sentences about the information you found.

Boris isn't from Mexico.

_____

_____

_____

_____

_____

_____

◼ C. PEOPLE IN THE NEWS *Bring in pictures of people in the news: athletes, politicians, actors and actresses, etc. In a group, talk about each person.*

EXAMPLE

This is Julia Roberts. She's from the United States. She's an actress. I think she's divorced. I think she's about thirty years old.

Cut out a picture of a person in the news. Write about the person.

D. STUDENT TO STUDENT

Student A: Look at sentences 1 to 10 below. Listen to Student B and circle the verb you hear.

Student B: Turn to page 181. Read sentences 1 to 10 to Student A.

Student A

1. He   **is   isn't**   a student.
2. She   **is   isn't**   at school.
3. We   **are   aren't**   from Russia.
4. **I'm   I'm not**   married.
5. You   **are   aren't**   in Room 2.
6. They   **are   aren't**   at work.
7. She   **is   isn't**   single.
8. **I'm   I'm not**   a student.
9. It   **is   isn't**   Monday.
10. They   **are   aren't**   from Japan.

Student B

11. She   **is   isn't**   married.
12. He   **is   isn't**   at work.
13. We   **are   aren't**   at school.
14. Boston   **is   isn't**   a city.
15. It   **is   isn't**   in Mexico.
16. She   **is   isn't**   from China.
17. **I'm   I'm not**   a teacher.
18. He   **is   isn't**   20 years old.
19. We   **are   aren't**   at school.
20. You   **are   aren't**   in class.

When you finish, **Student A** will read sentences 11 to 20 on page 181. **Student B** will circle the correct verb.

■ A. PRONOUNS *Rewrite these sentences with **he, she, it** or **they.***

1. Mary is a student.   *She is a student.* _____
2. Tom is at school. _____
3. Peter and John are students. _____
4. The teacher is here. _____
5. School is open. _____
6. Ana is single. _____
7. The book is on the desk. _____
8. Marc is at work. _____
9. Lisa and Kate are at school. _____
10. The windows are open. _____

■ B. CONTRACTIONS *Rewrite these sentences with a contraction.*

1. I am a student.   *I'm a student.* _____
2. I am not fifty. _____
3. She is married. _____
4. It is Friday. _____
5. They are married. _____
6. It is on the table. _____
7. He is not at work. _____
8. They are absent. _____
9. It is hot today. _____
10. They are not on the table. _____
11. I am not a teacher. _____
12. She is not in the class. _____

C. BE Complete these sentences with is, am, or are.

1. He ___is___ at school.

2. They _____ at home.

3. I _____ in class.

4. She _____ on the bus.

5. We _____ students.

6. Jack _____ a student.

7. They _____ not from India.

8. They _____ married.

9. Marie _____ single.

10. Tom _____ friendly.

11. I _____ not from New York.

12. It _____ on the desk.

13. I _____ twenty.

14. It _____ Saturday.

D. SHORT QUESTIONS AND ANSWERS

Match the questions and answers

1. ___C___ What's his first name?

2. _____ What's his last name?

3. _____ Where is he from?

4. _____ How old is he?

5. _____ Is he married?

6. _____ Is he a student?

a. Yes, he is.

b. No, he isn't.

c. Adam.

d. He's from Poland.

e. Wojcik.

f. He's 15.

Complete the questions.

1. ___What's her name___ ?   Marie.

2. _____ ?   Dorleans.

3. _____ ?   Haiti.

4. _____ ?   She's twenty.

5. _____ ?   Yes, she is.

6. _____ ?   Yes, she is.

Read this story about Lorena. Then, write a story about yourself. What's your name? Where are you from? Where do you live? Describe your family.

Me

My name is Lorena Ortiz. I am from Buga, Colombia. Buga is a small city in central Colombia. I am seventeen years old. I am studying English at college. I want to be a dentist.

I have a small family. I live with my mother and my grandmother. My mother is a supervisor in a factory. My grandmother is at home all day. My sister and I are students. We live in an apartment on Second Street.

Lorena Ortiz

WORLD MAP *Say your name and write it on the blackboard. The other students will find your country on a world map. Copy your classmates' names below.*

My classmates are:

_____   _____   _____

_____   _____   _____

_____   _____   _____

_____   _____   _____

_____   _____   _____

_____   _____   _____

_____   _____   _____

Grammar Summary

■ 1. Statements: *Be*

Affirmative

I	am	
We		in class.
You	are	
They		at home.
He		
She	is	at school.
It		

Negative

I	am not	
We		in class.
You	are not / aren't	
They		at home.
He		
She	is not / isn't	at school.
It		

■ 2. Contractions

I am → I'm		**Examples**
he is → he's		**I'm** a student.
she is → she's		**He's** in my class.
it is → it's		**She's** from Mexico.
you are → you're		**It's** a big country.
they are → they're		**You're** at school.
we are → we're		**They're** from Vietnam.
is not → isn't		**We're** students.
are not → aren't		She **isn't** here.
		They **aren't** here.

■ 3. *Yes/no questions*

Short Answers

Am I a student?	Yes, you are.	No, you aren't.	No, you're not.
Are you from Cuba?	Yes, I am.	No, I'm not.	
Is he sixteen?	Yes, he is.	No, he isn't.	No, he's not.
Is she at work?	Yes, she is.	No, she isn't.	No, she's not.
Is it Monday?	Yes, it is.	No, it isn't.	No, it's not.
Are we at school?	Yes, you are.	No, you aren't.	No, you're not.
Are you students?	Yes, we are.	No, we aren't.	No, we're not.
Are they married?	Yes, they are.	No, they aren't.	No, they're not.

2 My Classmates

Adjectives

■ A. ADJECTIVES
Adjectives describe a person, place, or thing. Repeat these adjectives after your teacher. Ask about any new words. Write each adjective under the correct picture.

beautiful   tired   handsome   friendly   intelligent   busy   thirsty   hungry

_____   _____   _____   _____

_____   _____   _____   _____

■ B. OPPOSITES *Match each adjective with its opposite.*

tall	old
happy	large
young	short
small	heavy
thin	sad

■ C. MORE OPPOSITES *Write the opposite of each adjective. Use the words on the right.*

1. clean   dirty _____   old

2. hard-working _____   dangerous

3. hot _____   quiet

4. safe _____   cold

5. noisy _____   shy

6. nervous _____   lazy

7. new _____   dirty ✓

8. talkative _____   poor

9. expensive _____   relaxed

10. rich _____   difficult

11. easy _____   cheap

■ D. DESCRIBE IT *Use an adjective to describe these things.*

1. The United States is _____ .

2. My car is _____ .

3. The students in this class are _____ .

4. This classroom is _____ .

5. My books are _____ .

6. The teacher is _____ .

7. My mother is _____ .

8. Canada is _____ .

9. The street outside this building is _____ .

10. English is _____ .

■ E. DESCRIBE YOURSELF *Choose five adjectives that describe **you!***

I'm

_____

_____

_____

_____

and _____!

F. LISTEN: PEOPLE AND PLACES *Listen to the tape and write four adjectives under each picture.*

tall	_____	_____
thin	_____	_____
_____	_____	_____
_____	_____	_____

Use the adjectives under each picture. Describe the people and the map.

> **EXAMPLE**
>
> Anna is tall and thin.   She's serious.

■ G. ANSWER *Answer these questions about the people and the map.*

1. Is Anna from Mexico?
2. Is she heavy?
3. Is she a good student?
4. Is she busy?
5. Are Edgar and Maria married?
6. Is it cold today?
7. Are they hungry?

8. Are they thirsty?
9. Is Mexico a large country?
10. Is Mexico cold all the time?
11. Are the people friendly?
12. Are you thirsty?
13. Are you friendly?
14. Are you tired?

■ H. OR QUESTIONS *Answer these questions.*

1. Are you talkative or quiet?
2. Are you lazy or hard-working?
3. Is your classroom hot or cold?
4. Are the students quiet or noisy?
5. Is English easy or difficult?

Ask more questions using **or.** *Ask about your teacher, your classroom, and the students in your class.*

■ A. MY CLASSMATES

Sit with a partner or in a small group. Use the adjectives below and write about students in your class. Then, read a few of your sentences to the class.

EXAMPLE

Phoung is handsome.

Yelena and Diana are intelligent.

HAPPY thin young busy

INTELLIGENT

hard-working

friendly talkative

TIRED TALL

■ B. THIS CITY

In a group, answer these questions about the city you are in now. What do you like about this city? What don't you like?

1. What's the name of this city?
2. Is it large?
3. What's the population?
4. What state or province is this city in?
5. Is it the capital?
6. Is this city clean?

7. Is this city safe in the daytime?
8. Is this city safe at night?
9. Is this city busy?
10. Is this city quiet?
11. Is this city hot today?
12. Are the people in this city friendly?

I like this city because it's _____.

I don't like this city because it's _____.

■ C. MY COUNTRY *Draw a simple map of your country. Show the capital and the city you are from. Complete or circle the correct information below.*

I'm from _____ . It's a **large**   **small**   country.

The capital of my country is _____ .

It's here, in the   **north**   **south**   **east**   **west**   **center.**

The capital of my country is   **big**   **small.**   It's   **noisy**   **quiet.**

The population of my country is about _____ .

I'm from _____ . (name of town)

My country is   **hot**   **cold**   **hot and cold.**

The people in my country are   **friendly**   **unfriendly.**

Tell your group or your class more about your country.

■■

D. STUDENT TO STUDENT *Sit with another student. Ask your partner questions using these adjectives. Circle your partner's answer.*

Are you happy or sad? → I'm (happy)

1. happy   sad
2. relaxed   nervous
3. lazy   hard-working
4. shy   talkative
5. tall   short   medium height
6. old   young   middle-aged

Practicing on Your Own

■ **A. MY SCHOOL** *Answer these questions about your school.*

1. Are you in school now?

   Yes, I am.
   _____

2. What's the name of your school?

   _____

3. Where is it?

   _____

4. Is your school old?

   _____

5. Is your school large?

   _____

6. Is your school busy?

   _____

7. Is your classroom large?

   _____

8. Is your classroom quiet?

    _____

9. Are the students friendly?

    _____

10. Are the students noisy?

    _____

■ B. MY CLASS *Put the words in these questions in the correct order. Then, answer the questions.*

1. you / Are / tired ?

    Are you tired? No, I'm not.
    _____

2. teacher / your / Is / busy ?

    _____

3. Is / class / large / your ?

    _____

4. friendly / Are / students / the ?

    _____

5. your / teacher / relaxed / Is ?

    _____

6. hungry / you / Are ?

    _____

7. students / Are / the / talkative ?

    _____

8. school / Is / your / noisy ?

    _____

9. classroom / small / Is / your ?

    _____

■ C. PEOPLE IN THE NEWS
Bring in pictures of people in the news: athletes, politicians, actors and actresses, etc. Write about two people. Use four or five adjectives.

> **EXAMPLE**
>
> This is Sean Connery. He's a movie actor. Sean Connery is old. He's tall. I think he's good looking. He's rich.

Sharing Our Stories

Gung wrote a story about his city in China. Read his story. Then, write about your city or country.

Zhengzhou

I am from China. China is a very large country with many, many people. I am from Zhengzhou. Zhengzhou is the capital of the state of Henan. It is a big city with about two million people. Zhengzhou is a busy city. It is the transportation center of China. The biggest railroad station in China is in my city. Trains come and go all day, every day.

Gung Liu

Having Fun with the Language

■ A. WHICH PICTURE? *Your teacher will put ten pictures from newspapers or magazines on the blackboard and number the pictures from 1 to 10. The people will all be male or all be female. The pictures will show people who are young, old, happy, sad, hungry, etc.*

One student will come to the front of the class and write down the number of one of the pictures, only showing the teacher. The other students will ask questions and try to guess the correct picture.

> **EXAMPLE**
>
> Is she old?   No, she isn't.
>
> Is she young?   Yes, she is.
>
> Is she happy?   Yes, she is.
>
> Is it number 6?   Yes, it is.

■ B. MY COUNTRY *Bring in pictures or postcards of your country or your city. Show the class the pictures and talk about them.*

Grammar Summary

■ 1. Adjectives

a. Adjectives describe a noun (a person, place, or thing).   **Example:** She's **tall**.

b. Adjectives are the same for both singular and plural words.   **Example:** She's **young**.
                                                                                  They're **young**.

c. Adjectives come **after** *be*.   **Example:** He is **busy**.

d. Adjectives also come **before** a noun (a person, place, or thing).   **Example:** He's a **busy** student.

■ 2. *Or questions*

Are you talkative *or* quiet?   I'm talkative.

Is Canada large *or* small?   It's large.

Are the windows clean *or* dirty?   They're clean.

3 The Classroom

Singular and Plural Nouns

 A. LISTEN: THE CLASSROOM *Listen to this classroom vocabulary. Write **a** or **an** for each word.*

1. ___*a*___ book
2. _____ student
3. _____ pencil
4. _____ umbrella
5. _____ notebook
6. _____ pen
7. _____ dictionary

8. _____ ruler
9. _____ eraser
10. _____ pencil sharpener
11. _____ man
12. _____ woman
13. _____ desk
14. _____ apple

15. _____ backpack
16. _____ chair
17. _____ computer
18. _____ map
19. _____ clock
20. _____ calculator
21. _____ teacher

Write the name of the classroom object under each item.

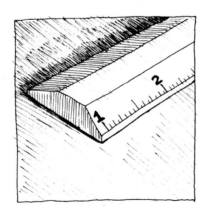

_____   _____   _____

22

  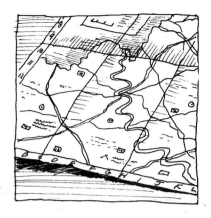

_____ _____ _____

■ B. A OR AN *Write a or an in each sentence.*

1. I'm ___a___ student.

2. I'm _____ excellent student.

3. He's _____ teacher.

4. He's _____ English teacher.

5. He's _____ good teacher.

6. This is _____ umbrella.

7. This is _____ easy lesson.

8. It's _____ cold day.

9. That's _____ dictionary.

10. That's _____ English dictionary.

11. She's _____ American.

12. I have _____ pencil.

13. I need _____ pencil sharpener.

14. This is _____ backpack.

■ C. SINGULAR OR PLURAL *Look around the classroom and tell your teacher the names of fifteen more classroom objects. Your teacher will write them on the board. Write the words under* **Singular** *or* **Plural**. *Remember to use* **a** *or* **an** *for all singular nouns.*

Singular | Plural

a calendar   desks
an outlet   wi
a door

D. LISTEN: SINGULAR OR PLURAL *Listen and circle the word you hear.*

1.	a book	books	6.	a door	doors
2.	a pencil	pencils	7.	a table	tables
3.	a student	students	8.	a dictionary	dictionaries
4.	a window	windows	9.	a man	men
5.	a clock	clocks	10.	a woman	women

E. MY CLASSMATES *Use these words and talk about students in your class.*

EXAMPLE

Mohammed is a hard-working person.

Ana and Lin are women.

NEW STUDENTS   a man   **men**

a friendly person

A TIRED STUDENT   **friendly people**

a talkative person

a serious student

excellent students

a student

AN INTELLIGENT STUDENT

women   *a woman*

a hard-working person

F. *THIS, THAT, THESE, THOSE* *Follow the examples in the pictures below and act out each sentence. Remember, you need to hold some objects. You need to point to other objects.*

1. This pencil is short.
2. This watch is expensive.
3. That book is heavy.
4. That jacket is nice.
5. That dictionary is big.
6. These books are old.
7. These keys are noisy.
8. These shoes are comfortable.
9. Those desks are small.
10. Those windows are closed.
11. This desk is clean and that desk is dirty.
12. This hat is old and that hat is new.
13. This table is small and that table is large.
14. These books are open and those books are closed.
15. These pencils are short and those pencils are long.

Having Fun with the Language

A. GUESS THE OWNER *Sit in a circle. Each student puts one object (for example: notebook, keys) in the middle of the floor or on a desk. Students pick up or point to an object and guess the owner.*

EXAMPLE

Roberto, is this your notebook?   No, it isn't.
Huasong, is this your notebook?   Yes, it is.
Elsa, are these your keys?   Yes, they are.

■ A. TIME *Write the correct time under each clock.*

three forty	three o'clock	three twenty
three fifteen	three forty-five	three fifty-five
three ten	three-oh-five	three thirty
three thirty-five	three fifty	three twenty-five

1. It's __three o'clock__ .

2. It's _____ .

3. It's _____ .

4. It's _____ .

5. It's _____ .

6. It's _____ .

7. It's _____ .

8. It's _____ .

9. It's _____ .

10. It's _____ .

11. It's _____ .

12. It's _____ .

■ A. TIME *Complete these sentences about yourself. Read them to a partner.*

1. This class begins at _____ .
2. This class ends at _____ .
3. The bank is open at _____ .
4. We are in school from _____ to _____ .
5. Our break is from _____ to _____ .
6. The post office is open from _____ to _____ .
7. I sleep from _____ to _____ .

Prepositions

at 3:00
at 11:30
from 8:00 **to** 10:00
from 9:00 **to** 5:00

B. STUDENT TO STUDENT

Student A: *Put different times on clocks 1 to 6. Student B will ask you the time. Do not look at your partner's book!*

Student B: *Ask Student A the time. Listen carefully and put the correct time on each clock.*

EXAMPLE

Student B: Clock 1. What time is it?
Student A: It's 6:15.
Student B listens and draws the time on the clock.

1.   2.   3.  4.

5.   6.  7.  8.

9.  10.  11.  12.

*When you finish, **Student B** will put different times on clocks 7 to 12, and then **Student A** will ask the time.*

■ A. SINGULAR OR PLURAL? *Complete these sentences with **is** or **are**. Use **a** or **an** if needed.*

1. He ___is a___ student.

2. They _____ students.

3. He _____ excellent student.

2. He _____ good student.

5. They _____ good students.

6. She _____ serious student.

7. He _____ tired student.

8. They ___are___ lazy students.

9. This _____ good book.

10. That _____ old book.

11. These _____ old books.

12. He _____ young man.

13. She _____ old woman.

14. They _____ good people.

■ B. ANSWER *Answer these questions. Use **it** or **they** in your answer.*

1. Is this your dictionary?
   ___Yes, it is.___

2. Are these your books?
   ___No,___

3. Is this your hat?
   ___No,___

4. Is that your umbrella?
   ___Yes,___

5. Are those your pencils?
   ___Yes,___

6. Are these your keys?
   ___No,___

7. Is this your pen?
   ___Yes,___

8. Is that your eraser?
   ___No,___

■ C. WRITE THE TIME *Write the correct time under each clock.*

1. _____

2. _____

3. _____

4. _____

5. _____

6. _____

◼ 1. Singular and plural nouns

a. Use **a** before a singular count noun.
   a book   a pencil

b. Use **an** before a singular count noun that begins with a vowel sound (*a, e, i, o,* or *u*).
   an eraser   an hour   an excellent student

c. Use **s** for plural count nouns.
   two pencils   four books

d. Do not use **s** for adjectives.
   My book is old.   My books are old.

◼ 2. *This, that, these, those*

a. Use **this** and **these** to talk about objects that are near you.
   This book is interesting.   **These** books are heavy.

b. Use **that** and **those** to talk about objects that are not near you.
   That student is intelligent.   **Those** students are busy.

◼ 3. Spelling

Noun ending	→	Spelling
1. Most nouns	→	Add **s**
pen		pens
girl		girls
boy		boys
2. Nouns that end with **ch, sh, ss, x, zz**	→	Add **es**
watch		watches
class		classes
3. Nouns that end with a consonant and **y**	→	Change the **y** to **i**, add **es**
city		cities
dictionary		dictionaries
4. Irregulars	→	Memorize!
man		men
woman		women
person		people
child		children

4 The Family

Possessive Nouns

A. FAMILY RELATIONSHIPS *Repeat these words after your teacher. Ask about any new words.*

wife	husband	aunt	uncle
mother	father	niece	nephew
daughter	son	grandmother	grandfather
sister	brother	granddaughter	grandson

■■■

B. LISTEN: FAMILY RELATIONSHIPS *Listen to the tape and fill in the family relationships.*

1. Pedro is Rosa's _____husband_____.

2. David is Pedro and Rosa's _____.

3. David is Stella's _____.

4. Stella is Rosa's _____.

5. Olga is Tom's _____.

6. Kathy is Tom's _____.

7. Stella is Tom and Kathy's _____.

8. Tom is Stella's _____.

■ C. DESCRIBE FAMILY RELATIONSHIPS *Talk about the relationships in the Garcia family. Give two or more relationships for each person.*

EXAMPLE

Stella is Kathy's aunt.   Stella is David's sister.

Stella Rosa	is	Kathy's Rosa's David's	aunt. daughter. mother. sister.
Pedro and Rosa Tom and Kathy	are	Stella and David's Tom and Kathy's Olga and David's	grandmother. grandparents. parents. children.

■ D. ANSWER *Answer these questions about the Garcia family.*

EXAMPLE

Who is Tom's sister?   Kathy is.

1. Who is Pedro's wife?
2. Who is Rosa's son?
3. Who is Pedro and Rosa's daughter?
4. Who is Stella's brother?
5. Who is David and Olga's son?

6. Who is Kathy's brother?
7. Who is David's father?
8. Who is Pedro and Rosa's grandson?
9. Who is Tom's aunt?
10. Who is Stella's niece?

my   your   his   her   our   their

E. LISTEN: POSSESSIVE ADJECTIVES

*Listen to the tape and complete these sentences with **she** or **her.***

1. This is my little sister.

2. __Her_____ name is Maria.

3. _____'s sixteen years old today, but _____ birthday is next week.

4. _____ eyes are brown and _____ hair is long and brown.

5. _____'s in tenth grade.

*Listen to the tape and complete these sentences with **he** or **his.***

1. This is my brother.

2. _____ name is David.

3. _____'s nineteen years old and _____'s in college.

4. _____ birthday is on October 2nd.

5. _____'s on the baseball team.

*Listen to the tape and complete these sentences with **they** or **their.***

1. This is my brother Steve and his wife, Sue.

2. _____'re married and _____ live in Florida.

3. _____ home is in Miami.

4. _____ have two children. _____ names are Brian and Kevin.

◼ F. PERSONAL INFORMATION *Answer these questions about the drivers' licenses.*

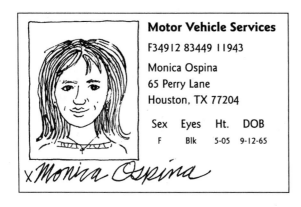

Motor Vehicle Services

F34912 83449 11943

Monica Ospina
65 Perry Lane
Houston, TX 77204

Sex	Eyes	Ht.	DOB
F	Blk	5-05	9-12-65

x *Monica Ospina*

1. What's her first name?
2. What's her last name?
3. What's her address?
4. What's her date of birth?
5. How old is she?
6. What is her height?
7. What color are her eyes?

Motor Vehicle Services

N2984 05743 48596

Mehmet Kose
225 Wall Street
Seattle, WA 98145

Sex	Eyes	Ht.	DOB
M	Br	5-10	6-21-80

x *Mehmet Kose*

1. What's his first name?
2. What's his last name?
3. What's his address?
4. What's his date of birth?
5. How old is he?
6. What's his height?
7. What color are his eyes?

◼ G. CLASSMATES *Write the name of a student in your class who matches each description. Then write the sentence again with **his** or **her**.*

1. ____Maria's____ hair is black. → 1. ___Her___ hair is black.

2. _____ eyes are brown. → 2. _____ eyes are brown.

3. _____ hair is brown. → 3. _____ hair is brown.

4. _____ eyes are blue. → 4. _____ eyes are blue.

5. _____ eyes are large. → 5. _____ eyes are large.

6. _____ hair is long. → 6. _____ hair is long.

7. _____ hair is curly. → 7. _____ hair is curly.

8. _____ hair is short. → 8. _____ hair is short.

A. OCCUPATIONS *Repeat these occupations after your teacher. Ask about any new words.*

a cook   a waiter / a waitress   police officers   an accountant

a custodian   factory workers   an engineer   a housewife

Match the occupation and the picture.

factory workers   a housewife   police officers   a cook

a waitress   an accountant   an engineer   a custodian

B. MORE OCCUPATIONS *These are the names of twelve more jobs. Repeat them after your teacher and ask about any new words.*

a nurse	a secretary	a machine operator
a nurse's aide	a teacher	a computer programmer
a bartender	a dentist	a bus driver
a landscaper	a farmer	a mail carrier

Talk about the people in your family. What are their occupations?

EXAMPLE

My brother is a cook.

My mother is a mail carrier.

■ C. WORK PLACES *Write occupations from exercises* **A.** *and* **B.** *under each category.*

Hospital	Office	Factory
nurse	dentist	custodian
nurse's aide	engineer	factory worker
custodian	accountant	computer programmer
	secretary	machine operator
	custodian	

Restaurant	School	Outside
waiter,	teacher	farmer
cook	custodian	police officer
bartender	nurse	bus driver
	secretary	landscaper
		mail carrier

■ D. A AND AN *Put* **a** *or* **an** *before each occupation.*

1. __a__ nurse

2. __a__ landscaper

3. __a__ tired secretary

4. __a__ doctor

5. __a__ police officer

6. __an__ excellent dentist

7. __an__ engineer

8. __an__ accountant

9. __a__ busy waitress

Having Fun with Language

■ ✂ A FAMILY TREE *Cut out the pictures on page 179. Give each person a name. Then, make a family tree. Do not let your partner see how you arrange your pictures to make a family tree. Talk about the family and describe the relationships. Your partner will try to arrange the family tree the same way.*

Working Together

■ A. MY FAMILY *Draw a picture of your family. Use stick figures. Write each person's name. Tell your group about your family and the different relationships.*

D. STUDENT TO STUDENT

Student A: *Ask Student B the questions about the young woman below. Write the answers.*

Student B: *Turn to page 182 and look at the list of answers. Student A will ask you questions. The answers are not in order. Give your partner the correct answer from your list.*

1. What's her first name? _____

2. What's her last name? _____

3. How old is she? _____

4. When is her birthday? _____

5. What's her occupation? _____

6. Where is she from? _____

7. What color is her hair? _____

8. What color are her eyes? _____

*When you finish, **Student B** will ask the questions and **Student A** will give the answers from page 182.*

■ C. PHOTOGRAPHS *Two students, Mira and Nellie, are talking about photographs of their family. With a partner, read and practice the conversation below.*

Mira: These are my brothers, Peter and Marek. Peter is 8 and Marek is 16.

Nellie: Are they in school?

Mira: Peter is in third grade. Marek is in high school. He's in tenth grade. And how about you?

Nellie: I have a little girl. This is her picture. Her name is Jenny.

Mira: She's beautiful. How old is she?

Nellie: She's nine months.

Mira: She looks like you. She has your eyes and mouth.

*Bring in one or two photographs of your family. Write a conversation with a partner. Use the **Helpful Language** below. Present your conversation to a small group or to the class.*

Helpful Language

Who's this?	Who's this?
What's his name?	What's her name?
How old is he?	How old is she?
Is he in school?	Is she in school?
What's his occupation?	What's her occupation?
He looks like you.	She looks like you.
He looks like his father.	She looks like her father.
He has your eyes / hair / smile.	She has your eyes / hair / smile.

A. WRITE ABOUT YOURSELF *Answer these questions about yourself.*

1. What's your first name?

   My first name is . . .

2. What's your last name?

3. What's your date of birth?

4. What's your address?

5. What's your occupation?

6. What's your height?

7. What color is your hair?

8. What color are your eyes?

9. What's your mother's name?

10. What's your father's name?

■ B. FAMILY RELATIONSHIPS *Complete these sentences about the Carter family tree*

1. Roger is Sylvia's _____husband_____ .

2. Richard is Roger's _____ .

3. Leslie is Roger's _____ .

4. Leslie is Richard's _____ .

5. Leslie is Deron's _____ .

6. Will is Jessica's _____ .

7. Sylvia is Michael's _____ .

8. Will is Sylvia's _____ .

9. Richard is Jessica's _____ .

10. Michael is Richard's _____ .

■ C. THE CARTER FAMILY *Use the information in the family tree to write about the Carter family.*

This is the Carter family. Roger and Sylvia live in Chicago, Illinois. _____They_____ have two children. Leslie is _____ years old. _____ _____ married to _____ and they live in San Diego, California. Leslie is a nurse in a school. Deron, _____ husband, is a police officer. They have three _____ , a _____ and two _____ . Jessica is _____ years old. _____ _____ in fourth grade. Will is _____ years old. _____ _____ in second grade. Michael is _____ _____ old and _____'s in nursery school. Roger and Sylvia have another _____ . _____ name is Richard and he's _____ years _____ . He's going to get married this summer.

NATALYA'S FAMILY *Read this story about Natalya's family. Then, write about your family. Where do you live? How many people are in your family? Write about your mother and father, brothers and sisters.*

My Family

My name is Natalya Zavalunova. I'm 23 years old. My family and I are from Tashkent, Uzbekistan. We live in an apartment in a large city. Many of our relatives live in the United States, too. My father, Daniel, has a brother and sister who live near us, and another sister lives in New York City. My mother, Olga, is a housewife. My father is an electrician. My sister, Tatyana, and I are college students. I am studying information systems and she is studying accounting and finance. My mother and father study English four evenings a week at the community college.

Natalya Zavalunova

Grammar Summary

▪ 1. Possessive nouns *Nouns: add an (') + s.*

Noun	Possessive	Examples:
Olga	Olga's	David is Olga's husband.
Tom	Tom's	That is Tom's book.
Tom and Kathy	Tom and Kathy's	David is Tom and Kathy's father.

▪ 2. Possessive adjectives *Use a possessive adjective before a noun.*

I	→	My	**My** class is at 9:00.
You	→	Your	**Your** hair is long.
He	→	His	**His** eyes are brown.
She	→	Her	**Her** pencil is yellow.
We	→	Our	**Our** teacher is friendly.
They	→	Their	**Their** classroom is hot.

5 The House

Prepositions

■ A. THE HOUSE

Repeat these words after the teacher. Ask about any new words.

stove	armchair	sink	night table	sofa
bed	bathtub	toilet	refrigerator	end table
television	pictures	chairs	coffee table	cabinets
light / lamp	shower	dresser	counter	table

Write the furniture under the correct room.

Bedroom	Bathroom	Living Room	Kitchen

■■

B. LISTEN: PREPOSITIONS *Listen and write the preposition you hear.*

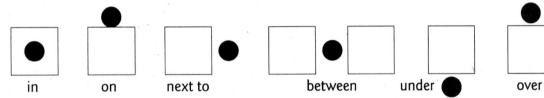

in   on   next to   between   under   over

1. The sofa is __in__ the living room.

2. The end table is _____ the sofa.

3. The books are _____ the coffee table.

4. The lamp is _____ the end table.

5. The picture is _____ the sofa.

6. The dresser is _____ the bedroom.

7. The night table is _____ the bed and the dresser.

8. The shoes are _____ the bed.

9. The table is _____ the kitchen.

10. The basket is _____ the sink.

11. The window is _____ the sink.

12. The cabinets are _____ the refrigerator.

13. The cat is _____ the chair.

14. The remote control is _____ the table.

 C. ANSWER *Answer these questions about the items in this house.*

> **EXAMPLE**
>
> Where is the end table?   It's next to the sofa.
>
> Where are the books?   They're on the coffee table.

1. Where is the television? It's on the table

2. Where is the refrigerator? Its next to the fridge.

3. Where is the picture? It's over the sofa

4. Where is the sofa? It's

5. Where is the night table?

6. Where are the cabinets?

7. Where is the cat?

8. Where is the toilet?

9. Where is the bathtub?

10. Where are the shoes?

41

■ A. THE BEDROOM *Put the number of each item in the correct location in the bedroom.*

1. Put a clock radio on the dresser in the bedroom.
2. Put a small photo next to the clock radio, on the right.
3. Put a mirror over the dresser.
4. Put a box of tissues on the night table.
5. Put a calendar on the wall.
6. Put a tennis racket next to the dresser on the right.
7. Put two books on the floor next to the bed.
8. Put a window next to the bed on the left.

B. STUDENT TO STUDENT

*Student A: Listen to Student B read seven sentences about this kitchen. Circle **Yes** or **No**.*

Student B: Turn to page 182 and read the sentences to Student A.

1. Yes   No
2. Yes   No
3. Yes   No
4. Yes   No
5. Yes   No
6. Yes   No
7. Yes   No

When you finish, **Student A** will read the sentences on page 182 and **Student B** will circle **Yes** or **No**.

C. THE CLASSROOM *Look around your classroom and answer these questions with a partner.*

1. Where is the door?
2. Where are the windows?
3. Where is the clock?
4. Where is the teacher?
5. Where is the teacher's desk?

6. Where is the chalkboard?
7. Where is the wastepaper basket?
8. Where is the map?
9. Where are you?
10. Where is your friend?

D. INTERVIEW *Ask your partner these questions. Circle **Yes** or **No.** Write the location for the **Yes** answers.*

EXAMPLE

Do you have a stereo? Yes.

Where is it? It's in the living room.

Question	Yes	No	Location
1. Do you have a stereo?	Yes	No	
2. Do you have a computer?	Yes	No	
3. Do you have a CD player?	Yes	No	
4. Do you have a VCR?	Yes	No	
5. Do you have a microwave?	Yes	No	
6. Do you have a calendar?	Yes	No	
7. Do you have an alarm clock?	Yes	No	

E. WHO HAS WHAT? *This chart shows the percentage of homes with different kinds of electronic equipment. Look at the chart and complete these sentences. There are many possible answers.*

1. Most homes have a / an _____ .

2. Many homes have a / an _____ .

3. Not many homes have a / an _____ .

4. _____% of homes have a / an _____ .

5. A / an _____ is more popular than
   a / an _____ .

6. A / an _____ is one of the most
   popular electronic products.

7. I would like to have a / an _____ .

Electronic Equipment	
Television	98%
Radio	98%
Telephone	96%
VCR	88%
Answering machine	60%
Personal computer	40%
Camcorder	23%
Fax machine	8%

43

Barbara is writing about her daughter's bedroom. Read her story and her daughter's response. Then, write about your bedroom. Is it neat or messy? What's in your bedroom? What color is it? What's on the walls?

Barbara: My daughter is 15 years old. This is a picture of her bedroom. It's very messy! Her clothes are on the floor. Look at her bed! Her clothes and her books and her telephone are on the bed. "Clean your room, Megan."

Megan: This is my room. I love it! Everything is in the right place. I know my clothes are on the floor, but they're clean. I know where everything is. This is my room. I like it this way.

Practicing on Your Own

 A. PREPOSITIONS *Look at the house on page 40 and write the correct preposition.*

1. The dresser is _____in_____ the bedroom.

2. The shoes are _____ the bed.

3. The lights are _____ the bed.

4. The dresser is _____ the night table.

5. The toilet is _____ the bathroom.

6. It is _____ the bathtub and the sink.

7. The bathroom is _____ the bedroom.

in
on
next to
under
over
between

8. The sofa is _____ the living room.

9. There is a picture _____ the sofa.

10. There is an end table _____ the sofa.

11. The kitchen is _____ the living room.

12. There is a toaster oven _____ the counter.

13. The cat is _____ the chair _____ the kitchen.

14. There is a basket _____ the sink.

15. The window is _____ the sink.

B. ANSWER *Bob's room is always a mess. Answer these questions about his things.*

1. Where's my soccer ball?   It's in your closet. _____

2. Where's my radio?   It's under your desk _____

3. Where's my belt? _____

4. Where's my tennis racket? _____

5. Where's my wallet? _____

6. Where's my calendar? _____

7. Where are my sneakers? _____

8. Where's my backpack? _____

9. Where's my tie? _____

10. Where's my telephone? _____

◼ C. WRITE ABOUT YOUR HOME *Answer these questions about yourself and your home or apartment.*

1. Where is your textbook? _____

2. Where is your pencil? _____

3. Where is your dictionary? _____

4. Where is your telephone? _____

5. Where is your television? _____

6. Where is your clock? _____

7. Where is your calendar? _____

8. Where is your stereo? _____

◼ D. QUESTIONS AND ANSWERS *Write a question and answer for each picture.*

1. Where _____ ?

_____ .

2. _____ ?

_____ .

3. _____ ?

_____ .

GREAT ART *Draw a very simple picture with four or five objects on a piece of blank paper. Describe the picture in five or six sentences. After this, give the sentences to a partner, but do not give your partner the picture! Your partner will follow your directions and try to draw the picture. Then, compare your finished pictures.*

> **EXAMPLE**
>
> Draw a house.
>
> Put a child looking out a window.
>
> Put a car next to the house on the right.
>
> Put a tree next to the house on the left.
>
> Draw four clouds in the sky.
>
> Draw an airplane in the sky.

Grammar Summary

1. Prepositions

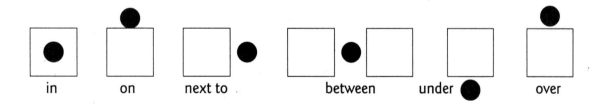

| in | on | next to | between | under | over |

2. *Where* questions

Questions			Answers
Where	is	Susan?	. . . She's in the living room.
		the lamp?	. . . It's next to the sofa.
	are	the flowers?	. . . They're on the television.

6 Downtown

More Prepositions

A. DOWNTOWN *Repeat the names of these stores and buildings after your teacher. Ask about any new words.*

department store	drugstore	bank	diner
supermarket	library	jewelry store	police station
laundromat	post office	barber shop	bookstore

Write the name of the store or building under the correct picture.

_____

_____

_____

_____

_____

_____

■■

B. LISTEN: STORES *Listen and write the name of the store in each sentence.*

1. Jae Hoon is at the ___bookstore___ .

2. Esperanza is at the _____ .

3. Marek and Beata are at the _____ .

4. Brian is at the _____ .

5. Lisa is on Main Street, at the _____ .

6. Mr. and Mrs. Garcia are at the _____ .

7. Sara is at the _____ .

■■

C. LISTEN: LOCATIONS *Listen to the location of each place and write it on the map below.*

1. laundromat   5. diner
2. park   6. drugstore
3. bank   7. police station
4. bus station   8. library

on   between   next to   on the corner of   across from

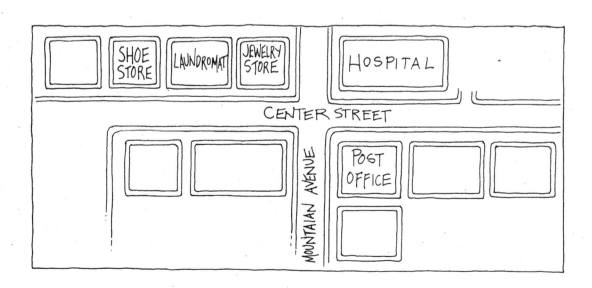

49

D. LOCATIONS *Describe the location of each place on the map on page 49.*

EXAMPLE

The post office is **across from** the hospital.

Working Together

A. STUDENT TO STUDENT

Student A: *Look at the map below. Ask Student B about the location of these places. Do not look at Student B's map.*

Student B: *Look at the map on page 183.*

the Mexican restaurant   the high school
the bus station   the diner
the bakery   the police station
the supermarket

EXAMPLE

A: Where's the Mexican restaurant?

B: It's on the corner of Second Street and River Road next to the barber.

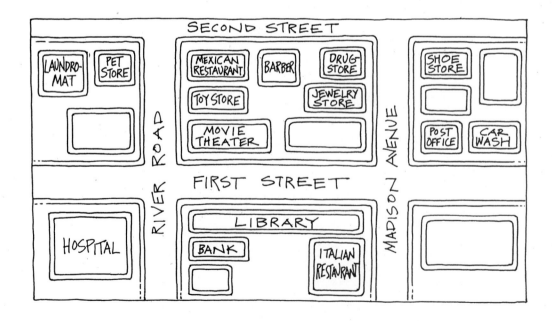

■ B. MY TOWN *Write the location of these buildings in your town.*

1. My school is _____ .

2. The post office is _____ .

3. The hospital is _____ .

4. The high school is _____ .

5. The police station is _____ .

Having Fun with the Language

■ ✄ A. A MAP *Sit with a partner. Cut out the pictures of the stores and buildings on page 179. Draw a street on a piece of paper. Place the buildings on your map, but do not let your partner see them (put a standing book between your desks). Describe the location of all the buildings and stores. Your partner will listen, ask questions, and try to arrange the downtown area the same way.*

Practicing on Your Own

■ A. COMPLETE THE MAP *Read the location of each store. Write the names of the stores on the map.*

		Post Office	Bank		

Broad Street

		Supermarket			

1. The **post office** is on Broad Street across from the supermarket.
2. The **bank** is between the post office and the bus station.
3. The **police station** is across from the bank.
4. There is a **laundromat** across from the bus station.
5. There is a **supermarket** between the barber shop and the police station.
6. The **high school** is on Broad Street next to the laundromat.
7. There's a **jewelry store** across from the barber shop.
8. The **shoe store** is next to the jewelry store and across from the library.
9. The **library** is on Broad Street across from the shoe store.
10. The **bus station** is between the bank and the diner.

■ B. PREPOSITIONS *Look at the map below. Fill in each blank with the correct preposition.*

on   on the corner of   next to
between   across from   near

1. The bank is _____ the jewelry store and the drugstore.

2. There is a bus station _____ the police station.

3. The high school is _____ Pine Avenue and Bay Street.

4. The library is _____ Bay Street.

5. The barber shop is _____ Pine Avenue and Bay Street.

6. There is a jewelry store _____ the laundromat.

7. The post office is _____ Pine Avenue.

8. The hospital is _____ the high school.

9. There is a shoe store _____ the bank.

10. The shoe store is _____ the barber shop and the library.

■ C. LOCATIONS *Where are these places? Look at the map above and complete these sentences.*

The drugstore is _____ .

There is a supermarket _____ .

The police station is _____ .

There is a diner _____ .

The laundromat is _____ .

NIMISHA AND ILA'S STORY *Neelam wrote a story about an area in her town, Edison, New Jersey. Write a story about the area you live in. Where do you live? Where do you shop? Where can you buy food and products from your country?*

This is a picture of a shopping area near our homes. We are from India, and we like to shop here because there are many Indian stores on this street. There are Indian groceries, bakeries, sari shops, jewelry shops, and there's also a hardware store and a video store. At the groceries, we can buy all of our favorite kinds of Indian pickles, like mango pickles and gajar pickles. The fruits from India are similar to the fruits in this country, and those are at the grocery, too. Many Indian men and women like to wear jewelry, especially gold. That's why there are so many jewelry shops on this street. Saturday and Sunday are the busiest days on this street.

Nimisha Patel and Ila Savia, India

Grammar Summary

■ Prepositions of place:

The jewelry store is **on** Park Avenue.

The bank is **next to** the drugstore.

The supermarket is **across from** the police station.

The bakery is **between** the shoe store and the post office.

The diner is **on the corner of** Main Street and Park Avenue.

A Typical Day

Present Tense

 A. LISTEN: A DAILY SCHEDULE *Listen to the story about a typical day for Susan and Paul. Write the time on each clock.*

B. LISTEN: PRESENT TENSE *Listen and write the present tense verb you hear.*

1. Susan and Paul ____*get*____ up at 7:00.
6. They _____ to school.

| They work |
| Susan works. |

2. They _____ breakfast at 7:30.
7. Susan _____ nursing.

3. Susan _____ to work.
8. After class, Susan _____ .

4. Paul _____ to work.
9. Paul _____ TV.

5. Paul _____ 15 miles from home.
10. They _____ to sleep at 12:00.

Listen to the story again. What other information do you remember about Susan and Paul?

■ C. DAILY SCHEDULES *Make statements about your schedule and Susan and Paul's schedule.*

I Susan and Paul	get up work eat lunch study	at _____ .
Susan Paul	gets up works eats lunch studies	from _____ to _____ .

■ D. CORRECT IT! *This information is not correct. Find the mistakes. Then, say the sentences correctly.*

I		
You		
We	**don't**	
They		work.
He		
She	**doesn't**	
It		

EXAMPLE

Susan drinks **coffee** in the morning.   They leave for work **at 9:00.**
Susan **doesn't drink coffee.**   They **don't leave at 9:00.**
She drinks **tea.**   They leave **at 8:00.**

1. Susan and Paul get up at 8:00.
6. They eat lunch at 6:00.

2. They eat breakfast at 7:00.
7. Susan studies typing.

3. Paul drinks tea for breakfast.
8. After class, Susan watches TV.

4. Susan drives to work.
9. After class, Paul studies.

5. Paul works from 9:00 to 4:00.
10. They go to bed at 11:00.

■ E. TIME EXPRESSIONS *Repeat these time expressions after your teacher. Ask about any new words.*

on	in	useful phrases
on Monday	in the morning	once a week
on Tuesday	in the afternoon	twice a month
on the weekends	in the evening	three times a day
	in the summer	every day

Talk about these activities using one of the time expressions.

EXAMPLE

I sleep late on Sunday.

I sleep late in the summer.

take a vacation

sleep late

take a walk

relax

RENT A VIDEO

WATCH TV

visit friends

read

take a long, hot bath

go to the beach

A. INTERVIEW *Sit with a partner. Ask and answer these questions and write the time.*

Question	You	Your partner
What time do you get up?		
When do you eat breakfast?		
What time do you go to school?		
What time do you get home from school?		
What hours do you work?		
What time do you get home from work?		
When do you eat dinner?		
What time do you do your homework?		
When do you relax?		
When do you go to sleep?		

B. MORE ABOUT THE INTERVIEW *Look at your chart and circle the correct information about your schedules.*

1. My partner gets up   **early**   **late**.

2. I   **get up**   **don't get up**   early.

3. My partner   **eats**   **doesn't eat**   breakfast.

4. I   **eat**   **don't eat**   breakfast.

5. My partner   **works**   **doesn't work**.

6. I   **work**   **don't work**.

7. My partner does homework in the   **morning**   **afternoon**   **evening**.

8. I do my homework in the   **morning**   **afternoon**   **evening**.

9. My partner   **relaxes**   **doesn't relax**.

10. My partner   **goes**   **doesn't go**   to bed at midnight.

C. STUDENT TO STUDENT

Student A: *Turn to page 183. Read the seven sentences to your partner.*

Student B: *Listen to Student A read seven sentences to you. If the statement is* true, *write* **True** *on the line. If the statement is* false, *write the correct information.*

> **EXAMPLE**
>
> **Student A:** Our class begins at 9:00.
>
> **Student B** (writes): *Our class begins at 10:00.*

1. _____

2. _____

3. _____

4. _____

5. _____

6. _____

7. _____

When you finish, **Student B** *will read seven new sentences on page 183 and* **Student A** *will write the correct information.*

Practicing on Your Own

A. PRESENT TENSE VERBS *Read about Susan and Paul's day. Circle the correct verb in each sentence.*

1. Susan   **get up**   (**gets up**)   at 7:00.

2. They   **eat**   **eats**   breakfast at 7:30.

3. Paul   **drink**   **drinks**   two cups of coffee every morning.

4. They   **leave**   **leaves**   for work at 8:00.

5. Susan   **walk**   **walks**   to work when it's nice out.

6. When it's raining, Susan   **don't walk**   **doesn't walk.**

7. Her friend   **give**   **gives**   her a ride.

8. Paul   **drive**   **drives**   because he lives 15 miles from his factory.

9. They **go** **goes** to school in the evening.

10. They **is** **are** tired at midnight!

B. MORE PRESENT TENSE VERBS *Complete each sentence with the correct form of the verb.*

eat	bring	buy	drink
get	have	stop	cook

1. Susan and Paul _____ *get* _____ up at 7:00 in the morning.

2. They _____ a small breakfast.

3. Paul _____ coffee in the morning.

4. Susan _____ tea.

5. Paul _____ at the store on the way to work.

6. He _____ another cup of coffee and a donut.

7. Susan _____ her lunch to work to save money.

8. Paul _____ in the cafeteria with his coworkers.

9. They _____ a small dinner on Monday and Wednesday.

10. Susan _____ dinner on Tuesday and Paul _____

dinner on Thursday.

C. TIME EXPRESSIONS *Use a time expression and complete these sentences about yourself.*

1. I get up _____ .

2. I go to school _____ .

3. I don't go to school _____ .

4. I work _____ .

5. I do my homework _____ .

6. I take a walk _____ .

7. I sleep late _____ .

8. I exercise _____ .

9. I watch TV _____ .

10. I go to the park _____ .

on
on Monday
on Tuesday
on the weekends

in
in the morning
in the afternoon
in the evening
in the summer

useful phrases
once a week
twice a month
three times a day
every day

■ D. WHAT DO YOU DO WHEN . . . . . ? *Match the sentence halves. You can match more than one!*

1. When I'm cold,   I take a long, hot bath.
2. When I'm happy,   I turn on the fan.
3. When I'm tired,   I drink a cup of hot chocolate.
4. When I'm hot,   I call up a friend.
5. When I'm lonely,   I sing.

Complete these sentences.

surprised

angry

bored

1. When I'm surprised, _____ .

2. When I'm angry, _____ .

3. When I'm nervous, _____ .

4. When I'm hungry, _____ .

5. When I'm bored, _____ .

Having Fun with the Language

■ A. GUESS! *Sit with a partner. Make guesses about your partner by writing a word on each blank. Then, read each guess to your partner. Your partner will tell you if you are right or wrong.*

A: I think you get up at 7:00 in the morning.   B: You're right.

A: I think you drink coffee for breakfast.   B: You're wrong. I don't drink coffee. I drink tea.

	My guess was	**Right**	**Wrong**

1. I think you get up at _____ .   ❑   ❑

2. I think you drink _____ for breakfast.   ❑   ❑

3. I think you _____ to school.   ❑   ❑
   (walk, drive, etc.)

4. I think you live _____ minutes from school.   ❑   ❑

5. I think you study _____ hours a day.   ❑   ❑

6. I think you watch TV _____ hours a day.   ❑   ❑

7. On the weekends, I think you like to _____ .   ❑   ❑
   (sport)

8. I think you go to bed at _____ .   ❑   ❑

9. I think you _____ .   ❑   ❑

10. I think you _____ .   ❑   ❑

■ B. MY DAY

The teacher will give each student ten small pieces of paper. On each, write an activity you do on a typical day, such as:

| brush my teeth | take a shower | study | eat breakfast | watch TV | get up |

It's not possible to write everything you do! Ten things are enough!

Then, give the pieces of paper to a partner and describe your typical day. Your partner will listen and arrange your papers in the correct order. The student who is speaking cannot touch the papers!

I get up at 6:30 in the morning. Next, I take a shower. Then, I brush my teeth.

Grammar Summary

■ 1. Simple present tense *Use the simple present tense to talk about routine actions. These actions happen every day, every weekend, every week, etc.*

■ 2. Statements

I We You They	work don't work	at 9:00.
He She It	works doesn't work.	from 9:00 to 5:00.

EXAMPLE

I get up at 7:00.

We don't go to school on Sunday.

He walks to school.

He doesn't have a car.

3. Spelling

Verb ending	→	Spelling
1. Most verbs	→	Add **s**
walk		walks
eat		eats
come		comes
2. Verbs that end with **ch, sh, ss, x, zz**	→	Add **es**
fix		fixes
brush		brushes
watch		watches
3. Verbs that end with a consonant and **y**	→	Change the **y** to **i**, add **es.**
study		studies
dry		dries
4. Exceptions	→	Memorize!
do		does
go		goes
have		has

 **Jobs**

Present Tense Questions

Grammar in Action

 A. LISTEN: JOB INFORMATION *Listen to Mateo and Ela talk about their jobs.*
Complete the information.

1. Mateo is a _____waiter_____ .

2. He works at a _____ .

3. He works _____ days a week.

4. He works from _____ to _____ .

5. He works _____ tables.

6. He _____ and

   _____ .

7. He often speaks _____ .

1. Ela is a _____ .

2. She works at a _____ .

3. She works _____ days a week .

4. She works from _____ to _____ .

5. She _____ and

_____ .

6. She often speaks _____ .

7. She gets _____ vacation.

■ **B. ASK AND ANSWER** *Ask and answer these **do / does** questions about your job and Mateo's and Ela's jobs.*

EXAMPLE

Do you work?	**Does he work?**	**Does she work?**
Yes, I do.	Yes, he does.	Yes, she does.
No, I don't.	No, he doesn't.	No, she doesn't.

Do	you	work?
		work full time?
		work part time?
		speak English at work?
Does	Mateo Ela	get tips?
		use a computer?
		get good benefits?

■ **C. ANSWER** *Answer these questions about Mateo and Ela.*

Mateo

1. Where does Mateo work?
2. What does he do?
3. How many days a week does he work?
4. What hours does he work?
5. How many tables does he work?
6. What language does he speak at work?
7. Does he make a lot in tips?

Ela

8. Where does Ela work?
9. What does she do?
10. Does she work full time?
11. What hours does she work?
12. Does she make hotel reservations?
13. Does she only speak Polish?
14. Does she stand all day?

■ D. WHO QUESTIONS Answer these **Who** questions about work. Talk about yourself, Mateo, and Ela.

1. Who works full time?
2. Who works a lot of overtime?
3. Who works the most hours?
4. Who makes good tips?

5. Who stands all day?
6. Who speaks English at work?
7. Who probably wears a uniform?
8. Who works hard?

Working Together

■ A. MY JOB Tell your partner or your class about your job, or tell the class about someone you know who works.

I'm a _____ . I don't work.

I work at _____ .

I work **part time / full time.**

I work _____ days a week.

I work from _____ to _____ .

> I work.
> He / she works.
> They work.

■ B. JOBS Talk about the jobs on page 67.

What is this person's job?

Where does this person work?

What does he do? What does she do?

Do you think this person needs to speak English?

What tools or equipment does each person use?

Would you like this job? Why or why not?

67

◨ B. INTERVIEW *Ask two students about their jobs or the jobs they would like to have and complete this chart.*

Questions	Student 1	Student 2
Where do you work?		
How many days a week do you work?		
What hours do you work?		
Do you ever work overtime?		
Do you speak English at work?		
Do you wear a uniform?		
Do you like your job?		
Do you get medical benefits?		

Use the information in the chart to answer these **Who** *questions.*

1. Who works five or more days a week?
2. Who works longer?
3. Who works overtime?
4. Who speaks English at work?
5. Who wears a uniform to work?
6. Who likes his or her job?
7. Who gets medical benefits?

◨ C. JOB REQUIREMENTS *Check the things you have to do at work.*

- ❑ I have to punch in.
- ❑ I have to wear a uniform.
- ❑ I have to wear safety glasses.
- ❑ I have to use a machine.
- ❑ I have to use special tools.
- ❑ I have to use a computer.

- ❑ I have to speak English.
- ❑ I have to lift heavy things.
- ❑ I have to work overtime.
- ❑ I have to talk on the telephone.
- ❑ I have to drive.
- ❑ I have to _____.

Compare your list and a partner's list. Complete these sentences.

We both have to _____.

I have to _____, but my partner doesn't.

My partner has to _____, but I don't.

◼ D. CLASSIFIED ADS *Match the abbreviation and the meaning.*

exp.	part time
FT	preferred
pref.	experience
PT	full time

MANICURIST—Licensed, exp. with nail art. PT in busy salon. Must be available Saturdays. Apply in person. 378 Summit Avenue, Madison.

ROOFER—Residential work. Start immediately. Will train. Must have valid driver's license. Good pay. Call Dave 691-8076

RECEPTIONIST—Area medical practice, pleasant office. FT position, Mon.–Fri. 12:00 to 8:00. Strong phone and word processing skills. Bilingual pref. Call Helen 744-6232.

AUTO BODY REPAIR PERSON—Exp. in taping, sanding, painting, and light body work. Small shop. Medical benefits and two weeks vacation. Call George 453-8125.

Answer these questions about the classified ads above.

1. What is the job?
2. Is it part time or full time?
3. Is experience required?
4. What education is necessary?
5. Does the applicant need a car?
6. Does the applicant need a special license?
7. Does the applicant have to speak English well?
8. Does the job offer any benefits?
9. Who do you call or see about this job?

Look in the classified ad section of a newspaper. Cut out or copy two ads for jobs that you would like to have. Talk about these ads in your class.

◼ E. A GUEST SPEAKER *Your teacher will invite a guest or a person who works in your school into the classroom. Before the speaker arrives, your class should write ten or more questions you would like to ask the speaker. This person will tell you about his or her job. Then, ask the speaker the questions on your list.*

■ A. PRESENT TENSE Complete each sentence with the correct form of the verb in present tense. Some of the verbs are negative.

help	sell
use	speak
make	pay
work	get

1. Ling is a cashier at Kids' World. She ____works____ in a store.

2. The store _____ children's clothing.

3. The store _____ women's clothing.

4. She _____ from 1:00 to 9:00, six days a week.

5. Ling _____ the customers.

6. Sometimes she _____ English and sometimes she _____ Mandarin.

7. Most people _____ cash.

8. Some customers _____ their credit cards.

9. Ling _____ $7.00 an hour.

10. She _____ any tips.

■ B. QUESTIONS AND ANSWERS Put these words in the correct order and write questions about Ling's job. Then, write an answer to the question.

1. Ling / Where / work / does ?

   Where does Ling work _____ ?

   She works at Kids' World _____ .

2. hours a week / work / How many / does / she ?

   _____ ?

   _____ .

3. What / store / does / this / sell ?

_____ ?

_____ .

4. make / How much / she / does ?

_____ ?

_____ .

5. a cash register / use / Does / she ?

_____ ?

_____ .

6. language / speak / does / What / she ?

_____ ?

_____ .

7. most / Do / use / customers / cash ?

_____ ?

_____ .

■ C. QUESTIONS *Read this story about Ling's job. Then, write the questions.*

It's very busy today at Kids' World. It's the holiday season, so the store is crowded. Ling works at the cash register. Some days she likes her job and time passes quickly. Other days, time passes very slowly. Today Ling has a difficult customer. The woman wants to return a sweater, but she doesn't have the receipt. The line is getting long, and the other customers look angry. Here comes the store manager, Mrs. Robinson. Mrs. Robinson always takes care of the problems. Ling is very happy to see her.

1. Why __is the store busy today__? Because it's the holiday season.

2. Where _____? At the cash register.

3. Who _____? Ling does.

4. What _____? A sweater.

5. _____? No, she doesn't.

6. How _____? Angry.

7. Who _____? Mrs. Robinson does.

Taylan and Florence wrote about their jobs. Write about your job or the job of someone you know. Where do you work? What do you do? What hours do you work? Do you enjoy your job? Why / why not?

I work at Sunset Fabrics. We sell fabrics, patterns, notions, buttons, lace—everything you need for sewing. I help the customers and I cut the fabrics. I have to cut the fabrics straight and we always give the customer three or four inches extra. I go to school in the morning, then I walk two blocks to the store. My hours are great. I work from 12:00 to 8:00, six days a week. The job is easy and light. Only four people work in the store and I like all of them. For me at this time, it is the perfect job.

Taylan Batuman

My name is Florence Joseph, and I'm from Haiti. I am a student worker in the ESL office at my college. I work part time from Monday to Thursday. My hours are from 4:30 to 7:30. I help the teachers and the students. I make photo-copies for the teachers and put their mail in their mailboxes. Students come into the office every day, so I have to answer a lot of questions. I also have to answer the telephone and take messages. I like my job because I meet a lot of new people, and it gives me more confidence in my English.

Florence Joseph

A. TWENTY QUESTIONS *Divide into groups of three to five students. Each group will decide on one occupation. One team will come to the front of the classroom. The other teams will ask* **Yes / No** *questions and try to guess the job. Listen to the answers carefully. Each team can only ask twenty questions.*

EXAMPLES

Do you work outside?   Do you help people?

Do you work at night?   Do you wear a uniform?

Is your job dangerous?   Is your job messy?

Do you work with children?   Do you work with your hands?

Grammar Summary: Simple Present Tense Questions

1. Yes/No questions

SHORT ANSWERS

	I	
Do	you	
	we	
	they	work?
	he	
Does	she	
	it	

. . . Yes, you do.   No, you don't.

. . . Yes, I do.   No, I don't.

. . . Yes, you do.   No, you don't.

. . . Yes, they do.   No, they don't.

. . . Yes, he does.   No, he doesn't.

. . . Yes, she does.   No, she doesn't.

. . . Yes, it does.   No, it doesn't.

2. Wh questions

		I	
Where		you	
	do	we	
When		they	work?
	does	he	
What hours		she	

Who questions (*Who* as subject)

Who	works	full time?

Who works full time? Mateo does.

Mateo and Ling do.

 **Food**

Count and Non-Count Nouns

■ A. FOOD *Repeat these food items after your teacher. Ask about any new words.*

apples	donuts	cookies	lettuce
spaghetti	ketchup	eggs	margarine / butter
rice	tomatoes	a lemon	oranges
bananas	a pie	ice cream	bread

Label the food in this kitchen.

74

◼ B. WHAT'S IN THE KITCHEN? *Use this chart and make sentences about the food in this kitchen.*

There	is	a	pie lemon pineapple	in the refrigerator.
		some	ice cream bread cereal rice	in the freezer. in the cabinet.
	are		eggs donuts oranges bananas	on the counter.

Count nouns
> a donut
> two donuts
> some donuts

Non-count nouns
> rice
> some rice
> milk
> some milk

C. LISTEN: COUNT AND NON-COUNT NOUNS *Listen and write the name of each food in the correct column.*

Singular Count	Plural count	Non-count
an apple	some apples	some rice

Write six more food items you know in English. Ask your teacher to help you with spelling. Add your favorite food items to the list above.

> Can you spell _____ ?
> How do you spell _____ ?

_____ _____ _____

_____ _____ _____

■ D. CONTAINERS *Look at the pictures and repeat these words after the teacher.*

box	bottle	can	bag	jar

_____ _____ _____ _____ _____

_____ _____ _____ _____ _____

_____ _____ _____ _____ _____

_____ _____ _____ _____ _____

Match the food with the container it comes in. Then add two more words to each list.

onions	mayonnaise	potato chips
soup	coffee	cereal
juice	soy sauce	spaghetti

■ E. LISTEN: A SHOPPING LIST *Listen to this couple talk about the food that they need at the supermarket. Circle the items they need. Cross out the items they don't need.*

apples	orange juice	toilet paper	spaghetti
bananas	apple juice	tissues	vegetables
oranges	chicken	paper towels	ice cream
pineapple	pork chops	cereal	
milk	beef	rice	

◼ A. FOOD ITEMS *Sit with a partner. Write and say the name of each food.*

a bag of onions   a bottle of soda

Talk about the information in the chart.

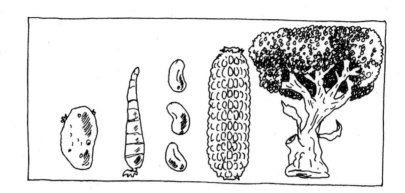

Adults' Favorite Vegetables	
Broccoli	20%
Corn	15%
Beans	12%
Carrots	11%
Potatoes	9%

The most popular vegetable for adults is _____ .

_____ is / are more popular than _____ .

Now talk about yourself.

1. I like _____ .

2. I don't like _____ .

3. My favorite vegetable is _____ .

Survey your class and find the five most popular vegetables. Each student can only pick one vegetable.

◼ **B. INTERVIEW** *Sit with a partner, and ask these questions about American food. Write* **Yes** *or* **No** *in each column.*

Question	You	Your Partner
Do you like hamburgers?		
Do you like hot dogs?		
Do you like french fries?		
Do like apple pie?		
Do you like rye bread?		
Do you like peanut butter?		
Do you like pizza?		
Do you like popcorn?		

Complete these sentences with information from your chart.

1. We both like _____ .

2. We both like _____ .

3. I like _____ , but my partner doesn't.

4. My partner likes _____ , but I don't.

■ C. COMPARING PRICES

*Visit a supermarket in your area. Choose a brand name you like and complete the information below. Then, compare your information in class. Use the **Helpful Language** box.*

Product and size	Brand name	Price
Toothpaste—4.6 ounces (oz)		
Rice—five pounds		
Orange juice—1/2 gallon		
Butter—1 pound (4 sticks)		
Soda, six-pack		
Salad dressing—8 oz.		
Toilet tissue—1 roll		
Bananas—1 pound		

HELPFUL LANGUAGE

I always buy _____ .

I never buy _____ .

I like _____ .

_____ is expensive.

_____ is cheap.

_____ is more expensive than _____ .

_____ is less expensive than _____ .

◼ A. *A, AN OR SOME* *Write* **a / an** *or* **some** *before each food item.*

1. _____ banana

2. _____ bananas

3. _____ onion

4. _____ onions

5. _____ bag of onions

6. _____ tomato

7. _____ tomatoes

8. _____ lettuce

9. _____ apple

10. _____ apples

11. _____ coffee

12. _____ can of coffee

13. _____ cup of coffee

14. _____ soda

15. _____ can of soda

16. _____ cookies

17. _____ box of cookies

18. _____ egg

19. _____ eggs

20. _____ bread

◼ B. COUNT AND NON-COUNT NOUNS *Complete these sentences with a verb, then use* **a, an,** *or* **some.**

1. There _____is_____ _____some_____ cereal in the cabinet.

2. There _____ _____ eggs in the refrigerator.

3. There _____ _____ popcorn in the microwave.

4. There _____ _____ banana on the counter.

5. There _____ _____ rice in the refrigerator.

6. There _____ _____ bread on the counter.

7. There _____ _____ orange on the counter.

8. There _____ _____ frozen pizza in the freezer.

9. There _____ _____ peanut butter in the cabinet.

10. There _____ _____ donut in the box.

■ C. THE CHECK-OUT COUNTER *What is Mrs. Gibson buying? Write seven sentences about her order.*

1.   She's buying two boxes of rice.

2.   _____

3.   _____

4.   _____

5.   _____

6.   _____

7.   _____

Having Fun with the Language

A. WHAT IS IT? *Your teacher will bring in seven paper lunch bags, each with a different food inside. The students will reach in without looking, feel the item, and then try to guess what it is. Your teacher will also try to think of some foods that may be different for you, such as raisins or an avocado.*

B. A TYPICAL FOOD *Each student will bring in a typical food item from his or her native country. It can be a fruit or a vegetable or a food in a can or box. Describe the food. Is it a fruit? Is it a vegetable? How does it grow? How do you prepare this food?*

C. HOW DO YOU MAKE RICE? *Three students from different countries (if possible) will describe how to make rice. Do all three students make rice the same way? What is different about their instructions? Ask students to write down their favorite recipes to give to each other in class. Hand out notecards to do this. Exchange recipes.*

Grammar Summary: Count and Non-count Nouns

1. Count and non-count nouns

a. Count nouns are things we can count. Count nouns can be singular or plural.

a donut   one donut   two donuts   three donuts   some donuts

b. Non-count nouns are things we can't count. We do not use the plural s with non-count nouns.

rice   some rice   oil   some oil   milk   some milk

c. We can put things in containers and count the containers.

a box of donuts   two boxes of donuts   a bag of rice   two bottles of oil

■ 2. There is, there are

There	is	a donut	in the kitchen.
		some rice	
		a box of donuts	
		a box of rice	
	are	five donuts	on the counter.
		some donuts	
		two boxes of rice	

The English Class

Present Continuous Tense

■ A. CLASSROOM ACTIVITIES *Repeat these verbs after your teacher. Ask about any new words.*

eat	drink	study	write	do	speak
walk	read	sit	stand	carry	sharpen

B. LISTEN: CLASSROOM ACTIVITIES
It's 8:55 and class begins at 9:00. These students are in the class a few minutes early. Listen and write the names on the correct person.

Carlos	Marc	Vin	Rosa	Linn
Ali	Maria	David	Adam	

C. LISTEN: PRESENT CONTINUOUS VERBS
Listen and write the verbs you hear.

1. Carlos _____is_____ _____talking_____ to Rosa.

2. He _____ _____ a donut.

3. Rosa _____ _____ a cup of coffee.

4. Carlos and Rosa _____ _____ in the classroom

5. Maria _____ _____ for a test.

6. Marc _____ _____ a book. He _____ _____ his homework.

7. Vin _____ _____ Vietnamese. He _____ _____ English.

8. The students _____ _____ French. They _____ _____ English.

> Carlos is talking.
> Rosa is talking.
> They're talking.

D. THE CLASSROOM
Make sentences about the classroom picture with the words in this chart.

Carlos		eating a banana.
Linn	is	drinking a cup of coffee.
David		talking.
Rosa	isn't	writing on the board.
		speaking Spanish.
Carlos and Rosa	are	sitting.
Vin and David	aren't	sharpening a pencil.

E. CORRECT IT!
This information is not correct. Look at the classroom picture and correct these sentences.

> **EXAMPLE**
>
> Linn is writing **the time** on the blackboard. Linn **isn't writing the time** on the blackboard. She's writing **the date** on the blackboard.

1. Carlos is eating an orange.

2. Rosa is drinking soda.

3. Carlos and Rosa are studying.

4. Ali is reading a book.

5. Maria is sitting with a friend.

6. Marc is sitting next to Rosa.

7. Vin and David are talking about soccer.

8. Vin and David are speaking Spanish.

■ A. MY CLASSROOM

Sit with a partner. Look around the classroom and complete these sentences with the name of a person in your class. Some of your answers can be **No one.**

1. _____ is standing.

2. _____ is writing.

3. _____ is sitting near the window.

4. _____ and _____ are talking.

5. _____ is speaking English.

6. _____ is speaking Vietnamese.

7. _____ is drinking a cup of coffee.

8. _____ and _____ are sitting near the door.

9. _____ is wearing sneakers.

10. _____ is sitting next to me.

WHAT'S HAPPENING AROUND THE SCHOOL?

Get into groups of two or three students. Decide to quietly sit or stand in one area of your school (for example, the cafeteria, the library, the main office, the front door, the parking lot, etc.). Now describe what is happening around you. Write seven sentences about what you see. Return to your class and write some of your sentences on the board.

1. _____

2. _____

3. _____

4. _____

5. _____

6. _____

7. _____

C. FAMOUS PEOPLE
Write the names of famous people in the chart below. Imagine what each person is doing now.

Category	Name	Action
The president of the U.S.	President	The President is talking on TV.
A politician		
A world leader		
An athlete		
An actor		
An actress		
A singer		

D. STUDENT TO STUDENT
Student A and Student B both have pictures of the same classroom. Do not look at one another's picture! There are seven differences in your pictures. Talk about your pictures and try to find the differences.

Student A: *Look at the picture below.*

Student B: *Turn to page 184. Look at the classroom picture.*

■ **A. CLOTHING** *Look at the students in your classroom. Check and talk about the items of clothing that people are wearing.*

_____ a shirt	_____ a belt	_____ panty hose
_____ pants	_____ a sweater	_____ sunglasses
_____ shorts	_____ a top	_____ earrings
_____ a dress	_____ jeans	_____ a ring
_____ a skirt	_____ a sweatshirt	_____ a necklace
_____ a blouse	_____ a T-shirt	_____ a chain
_____ a suit	_____ a hat	_____ a bracelet
_____ a jacket	_____ gloves	_____
_____ a coat	_____ socks	_____

Write the name of the article of clothing on the line under each item.

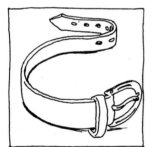   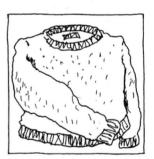

_____ _____ _____ _____

_____ _____ _____

◼ B. CLASSIFY: SINGULAR AND PLURAL *Look at the clothing vocabulary on page 88.*

Write seven more words in each column.

Singular	Singular (a pair of)	Plural
a dress	a pair of sneakers	sneakers
		earrings

◼ C. FIND SOMEONE WHO *Look around your classroom. Find someone who is wearing each item of clothing below.*

EXAMPLE

_____ is wearing _____ .

a skirt	a tie	long earrings	a ring
a sweatshirt	a jacket	a belt	socks
sneakers	a blouse	a T-shirt	a hat
brown shoes	shorts	a dress	glasses

D. GUESS WHO? *Look around the classroom. Describe one student's clothing, but do not use that student's name in your writing. Read your sentences to the class. The other students will guess the person you are describing.*

This student is wearing blue jeans and a white sweatshirt. He's wearing white sneakers.

He has a small gold earring in his right ear.

■ A. POSSESSIVE ADJECTIVES

The students in this picture are taking a break. Complete these sentences with a possessive adjective.

my   his   her   their

1. The students are taking _____their_____ break.

2. Vin is calling _____ son .

3. Ali and Rosa are doing _____ homework.

4. David is sharpening _____ pencil.

5. Adam is listening to _____ favorite tape.

6. Carlos is writing a letter to _____ girlfriend.

Subject pronoun	Possessive adjective
I	my
he	his
she	her
you	your
they	their

7. Linn is looking for change in _____ purse.

8. Maria is talking to _____ classmate, Linn.

9. Marc is talking to _____ wife. She's from another class.

10. I'm in the restroom. I'm washing _____ hands.

◼ B. PRESENT CONTINUOUS *Complete each sentence with an appropriate verb in the present continuous tense.*

1. Carlos ___is writing___ a letter to his girlfriend in Mexico.

2. Vin _____ in the hall. He _____ on the phone.

3. Adam _____ alone. He _____ to music.

4. Linn and Maria _____ at their desks. They _____ about their boyfriends.

5. Ali and Rosa _____ their homework. Rosa _____ vocabulary.

6. Marc _____ to his wife. He _____ under the clock.

7. The teacher _____ into the classroom. She _____ a cup of coffee.

◼ C. CONTRAST: PRESENT CONTINUOUS AND PRESENT *Read each sentence. If the sentence describes an action or event that is happening now, circle **Now**. If the sentence describes a routine action, circle **Routine**.*

1. Marc is talking to his wife.	(Now)	Routine
2. He talks to her at break time.	Now	Routine
3. Linn and Maria are talking.	Now	Routine
4. They talk about their boyfriends a lot.	Now	Routine
5. The teacher drinks five cups of coffee a day.	Now	Routine
6. She's drinking a cup of coffee.	Now	Routine
7. Adam is listening to his Walkman®.	Now	Routine
8. He listens to his Walkman at break every day.	Now	Routine
9. David is sharpening his pencil again.	Now	Routine
10. He sharpens it two or three times a day.	Now	Routine

D. MORE CONTRAST: PRESENT CONTINUOUS AND PRESENT

Complete these sentences with the correct form of the verb.

1. Vin _____is calling_____ his son. He _____calls_____

   him at break time every day. (call)

2. Rosa _____ earrings to class every day. Today she

   _____ a new pair. (wear)

3. Carlos _____ his girlfriend a letter today. He

   _____ her one letter a week. (write)

4. Marc _____ coffee almost every morning, but today he

   _____ soda. (drink)

5. Adam _____ to music all the time, but right now he

   _____ to the news. (listen)

Having Fun with the Language

A. FASHION SHOW
For the next class, wear your favorite clothes to class. You can also wear typical or traditional clothes from your country. Sit with a partner and describe one another's clothes in detail. Include color, length, material, and pattern. Your teacher will help you with new vocabulary.

After this, your partner will walk back and forth in front of the room. You play the announcer. Carefully describe your partner's outfit. One student can bring in soft music to play in the background.

Length	Material	Pattern	More Adjectives
long	cotton	striped	beautiful
short	wool	plaid	fantastic
	silk	flowered	wild
	leather	polka dot	great
		colorful	sophisticated

B. THE NEWS *Cut out a picture from a newspaper or magazine. Who is in the picture? What is happening? Describe the photo or event in two or three sentences.*

Grammar Summary

1. Present continuous tense *Use the present continuous tense to talk about what's happening now.*

2. Some present continuous time expressions

now   right now   at the present time

3. Statements

I	am am not	
He She It	is isn't	studying. working. talking.
We You They	are aren't	

4. Spelling

Verb ending	→ Spelling

1. Most verbs
    walk
    eat
    carry
	→ Add **ing**
	    walking
	    eating
	    carrying

2. Verbs that end with **e**
    write
    take
	→ Drop the **e** and add **ing**
	    writing
	    taking

3. One-syllable verbs that end with a consonant, vowel, consonant
    sit
    run
Do not double **x, y,** or **z**
    buy
	→ Double the final consonant and add **ing**
	
	    sitting
	    running
	
	    buying

A Fast Food Restaurant

Present Continuous Questions

■ A. A FAST FOOD RESTAURANT *Repeat these words after your teacher. Ask about any new words.*

work	pay	tray	uniform	call	hamburger
take	hand	cash register	in line	cry	
order	hold	counter	grill	cashier	

94

B. LISTEN: LUNCH TIME *Listen and write the name on the correct person in the fast food restaurant on page 94. Then talk about the picture. What is each person doing?*

Teresa	Tommy	Todd
Patty	Kim	Ken
Kathy	Jason	Ray

C. YES / NO QUESTIONS *Ask and answer questions about the people in this restaurant.*

Is he eating?	Is she eating?	Are they eating?
Yes, he is.	Yes, she is.	Yes, they are.
No, he isn't.	No, she isn't.	No, they aren't.

Is	Patty Kim Kathy	in line? ordering lunch? eating hamburgers? cooking hamburgers?
Are	Jason and Todd Ken and Ray	drinking a cup of coffee? working? talking?

D. LISTEN: QUESTIONS *Listen and write the question you hear. Then, circle the correct answer.*

1. Who is ordering lunch _____ ?

   a. Teresa is. b. A chicken sandwich. c. Patty is.

2. _____ ?

   a. Teresa is. b. She's working. c. She's ordering lunch.

3. _____ ?

   a. A hamburger. b. Ten dollars. c. A chicken sandwich.

4. _____ ?

   a. Yes, he is. b. He's eating. c. Because he's hungry.

5. _____ ?

   a. At the counter. b. In the kitchen. c. They're working hard.

95

A. FAST FOOD *Circle the fast food items that you like. Cross out the fast food items that you don't like.*

salad

apple pie

pizza **ONION RINGS**

CHICKEN PIECES

FRENCH FRIES

hamburgers   tacos

Compare your choices with your partner's and complete these sentences.

1. I like _____ and _____.

2. I don't like _____.

3. My partner likes _____ and I do, too.

4. My partner doesn't like _____ and I don't either.

5. We both like _____.

B. GROUP DISCUSSION *Sit in a group of four to five students. Talk about fast food restaurants using the questions below. Write the answers and report your information to the class.*

Question	Our Answers
1. Which fast food restaurants are in this area?	
2. Which one has a salad bar?	
3. Which one has the lowest prices?	
4. Which one has the best food?	
5. Which fast foods are high in fat?	
6. Which fast foods are good for you?	
7. Decide on a fast food restaurant for lunch. How much will lunch cost for your group?	

C. LISTEN TO PRICES   *Listen and write the prices you hear.*

1. __$.99_____   4. _____   7. _____

2. _____   5. _____   8. _____

3. _____   6. _____   9. _____

D. STUDENT TO STUDENT: MENU PRICES   *Ask about the price of each item and complete your menu.*

Student A: Look at the menu on page 185.

Student B: Look at the menu below.

$1.49 =	a dollar forty-nine
	one dollar and forty-nine cents
$3.50 =	three fifty
	three dollars and fifty cents

EXAMPLE

A: How much is a hamburger?

B: A dollar forty-nine.

Hamburger	$1.49	French fries	small	.99
Cheeseburger	1.79		large	1.39
Super Burger	2.99	Drink	small	
Chicken Sandwich			medium	
Fish Sandwich			large	1.39
Chicken Pieces	2.89	Coffee		
Salad bar		Apple pie		1.29

E. FIGURE OUT THE PRICE   *Look at the menu and figure out the total for each order.*

1. Boris is ordering dinner. He wants a super burger, large french fries, and a large soda. How much is his order?

2. Suni is at a fast food restaurant. She is ordering chicken pieces, the salad bar and a small drink. How much is her order?

3. Joseph is ordering two cheeseburgers, apple pie and coffee. How much is his order?

Write an order and read it to your group or your class. Who can figure out the correct total quickly?

■ A. YES / NO QUESTIONS

Crystal is a delivery truck driver. She and her partner are ordering lunch at a fast food drive in. Use the verbs below and complete these questions and answers in the present continuous tense.

take	sit	order	wait
talk	drive	wear	rain

1. _____Are_____ Crystal and her coworker at a drive-in window? _____Yes, they are_____ .

2. _____ she _____ a car? _____ .

3. _____ they _____ a lunch break? _____ .

4. _____ Crystal _____ a chicken sandwich? _____ .

5. _____ they _____ a hamburger? _____ .

6. _____ she _____ to the cashier? _____ .

7. _____ they _____ on a long line? _____ .

8. _____ they _____ their uniforms? _____ .

9. _____ they _____ inside the restaurant? _____ .

10. _____ it _____ today? _____ .

1. <u>What's Patty ordering</u>   ?

    She's ordering <u>a chicken sandwich</u>.

2. _____ ?

    She's standing <u>in front of the counter</u>.

3. _____ ?

    She's giving the cashier <u>ten dollars</u>.

4. _____ ?

    They're eating <u>hamburgers and french fries</u>.

5. _____ ?

    She's drinking <u>a cup of coffee</u>.

6. _____ ?

    They're talking about <u>their soccer game</u>.

7. _____ ?

They're working <u>in the kitchen</u>.

8. _____ ?

They're cooking <u>hamburgers</u>.

9. _____ ?

They're wearing <u>their uniforms</u>.

■ C. ASK QUESTIONS *Read the story and then write the questions.*

It's Easy to Make a Mistake

Teresa is a counter clerk at Mr. Burger. This is her first day at the cash register, and she's very nervous. She's working slowly and being careful not to make a mistake. The restaurant is getting busy and now there are six customers waiting in line. One man is getting impatient and he's making Teresa more nervous. Patty is at the register and Teresa is ringing up her order. Patty's order is $4.50 and she's handing Teresa a $10 bill. Teresa is giving Patty $6.50 in change!

1. Who _____is a counter clerk_____ ? Teresa is.

2. How many customers _____ ? Six.

3. Is _____ ? No, she's working slowly.

4. Who _____ ? One man is.

5. How much _____ ? $4.50.

6. How much change _____ ? $6.50.

Having Fun with the Language

A. LISTEN: ORDERING LUNCH
Listen to the conversation between a counter clerk and a customer. Fill in the missing words.

1: _____Can_____ I help you?

2: Sure. I'd like a _____ sandwich and a _____ .

1: What _____ soda—small, medium, or large?

2: _____ .

1: Anything else?

2: Ummm. A _____ fries.

1: That's it?

2: _____

1: For here or to go?

2: _____ .

1: That's a chicken sandwich, medium soda, and small fries. That's $ _____ .

Write a conversation with a partner. One student is a counter clerk and the other student is a customer.

B. THE PRICE IS RIGHT
Bring in a small item you bought recently, such as a tape, a calculator, a pair of earrings. The price must be ten dollars or less. Three classmates will guess the price.

That's $2.95.

That was $1.59.

You paid $4.50.

*The student who comes closest to the price, without going over the amount, is the **winner,** and shows the next item to the class.*

Grammar Summary

■ 1. Present continuous

    a. The present continuous talks about an action that is happening *now*.

    b. Time expressions: *now, right now, at this moment*

■ 2. *Yes/no questions*

Am I working?	. . . Yes, you are.	No, you aren't.	No, you're not.
Are you ordering?	. . . Yes, I am.	No, I'm not.	
Is he drinking a soda?	. . . Yes, he is.	No, he isn't.	No, he's not.
Is she waiting in line?	. . . Yes, she is.	No, she isn't.	No, she's not.
Is it working?	. . . Yes, it is.	No, it isn't.	No, it's not.
Are we paying?	. . . Yes, you are.	No, you aren't.	No, you're not.
Are you eating?	. . . Yes, we are.	No, we aren't.	No, we're not.
Are they cooking?	. . . Yes, they are.	No, they aren't.	No, they're not.

■ 3. *WH* questions

When	**am I**	working?	. . . Tomorrow from 4:00 to 9:00.
What	**are you**	ordering?	. . . A hamburger.
What	**is he**	drinking?	. . . A soda.
Why	**is she**	eating?	. . . Because she's hungry.
Where	**are we**	eating?	. . . At a restaurant.
Where	**are you**	walking?	. . . To a table.
What	**are they**	cooking?	. . . Chicken.

■ 4. Who questions (who as subject) *Who takes the singular verb form.*

Who is working at the counter?   Teresa is.

Who is working in the kitchen?   Kevin and Ray are.

Who	is	working?
		eating?
		paying?

12 The School

There Is / There Are

■ A. THE SCHOOL BUILDING *Repeat these words after your teacher. Ask about any new words.*

benches	flag	parking lot
garbage cans	mailbox	lights
water fountain	bus stop	statue
dogs	students	security guards
cars	pay telephone	security booth

■■■

B. LISTEN: THE SCHOOL *Listen to these sentences about the school and circle Yes or No.*

1. **Yes** No   3. **Yes** No   5. **Yes** No   7. **Yes** No

2. **Yes** No   4. **Yes** No   6. **Yes** No   8. **Yes** No

■■

C. LISTEN: QUANTIFIERS *Listen and complete these sentences with **is** or **are** and an expression from the box on the right.*

a
one
three
a few
several
some
a lot of
many
any

1. There ___is___ ___a___ telephone booth next to the building.

2. There _____ _____ bus at the bus stop.

3. There _____ _____ security guard in the booth.

4. There _____ _____ floors in the building.

5. There _____ _____ benches outside.

6. There _____ _____ students going into the building.

7. There _____ _____ garbage cans outside.

8. There _____ _____ students outside the building.

9. There _____ _____ cars in the parking lot.

10. There _____ _____ students at the bus stop.

■ D. *IS THERE / ARE THERE* *Answer these questions about the school buildings.*

EXAMPLE

Is there a flag outside?   Are there any lights in the parking lot?

Yes, there is.   Yes, there are.

No, there isn't.   No, there aren't.

1. Are there any baskets outside?   6. Is there a parking space?

2. Is there a guard in the security booth?   7. Are there any parking spaces?

3. Are there any students playing outside?   8. Is there a sign on the top of this building?

4. Are there any dogs outside?   9. Are there any students in front of the statue?

5. Is there a parking lot near the building?   10. Is there anyone in the telephone booth?

■ E. HOW MANY QUESTIONS *Ask and answer questions about the school building on page 104.*

> **EXAMPLE**
>
> How many cars are there in the parking lot?   There are a lot.
>
> How many trees are there outside?   There aren't any.

students	cars	benches	
dogs	bicycles	security guards	
mailboxes	doors	flags	

> There is one.
> There are two / three / four, etc.
> There are a few, several, etc.
> There are a lot.
> There aren't any.

■ F. QUESTIONS *Read the situation. Ask a question with* **Is there** *or* **Are there.**

> **EXAMPLE**
>
> You need to make a telephone call.   **Is there** a public telephone in this building?

1. You want to mail a letter.

2. You need to wash your hands.

3. You want to sharpen your pencil.

4. You would like a can of soda.

5. You would like a drink of water.

6. You need to make a copy of a paper.

7. You broke your foot and you are on crutches.

■ G. CIRCLE *Circle the correct word:* **there, they,** *or* **it.**

1. (There) They   are four students walking into the building. (They) There   are early.

2. **There It**   is a bus stop on campus. **There They**   aren't any students waiting for the bus. **There They**   are in class.

3. **There It**   is a mailbox in front of the building. **There It**   is full.

4. **There They** are several lights in the parking lot. **There They** aren't on now because it's daytime. **There They** are only on at night.

5. **There They** are many cars in the parking lot. **There They** are not students' cars. because this is a faculty parking lot. **There They** are four parking lots for students.

6. **There's It's** a telephone booth next to the building. **There's It's** empty.

7. **There It** is a statue in front of the building. **There It** is a statue of the founder.

8. **There They** are some students in front of the building. **There They** are relaxing between classes.

Working Together

■ A. OUR CLASSROOM *Sit with a partner and make statements about your classroom.*

EXAMPLE

There are four windows in our classroom.   *or*   There are a few windows in our classroom.

1. windows	4. desks	7. computers
2. maps	5. dictionaries	8. electrical outlets
3. students from _____ (country)	6. clocks	9. _____

■ B. *HOW MANY QUESTIONS* *Ask and answer questions about these items in the building you are in now.*

EXAMPLE

How many restrooms are in this building?   I think there are four.

1. elevators	4. vending machines	7. public telephones
2. restrooms	5. escalators	8. offices
3. classrooms	6. water fountains	9. _____

C. STUDENT TO STUDENT

Student A: *Turn to page 185. Read the eight sentences to your partner.*

Student B: *Listen to* **Student A.** *Write each sentence next to the correct picture.*

1. _____
   _____
   _____
2. _____
   _____
   _____
   _____

1. _____
   _____
   _____
2. _____
   _____
   _____
   _____

1. _____
   _____
   _____
2. _____
   _____
   _____
   _____

1. _____
   _____
   _____
2. _____
   _____
   _____

When you finish, **Student B** will turn to page 185 and read eight new sentences. **Student A** will then write them next to the correct pictures.

A. THE CLASSROOM *Complete these sentences about the students in your class.*

> There is one student.
> There are two / three / four / etc. students...
> There are a few students...
> There are many students...
> There aren't any students...

1. There __are_____ students in my class.

2. There _____ student(s) from Mexico.

3. There _____ student(s) from Japan.

4. There _____ student(s) from _____ .

5. There _____ man / men and _____ woman / women.

6. There _____ woman / women.

7. There _____ teenager(s).

8. There _____ teacher.

9. There _____ bus driver(s) in our class.

10. There _____ talkative student(s) in our class.

11. There _____ housewife / housewives in our class.

B. QUESTIONS *Circle the correct words in these questions and answers.*

1. A: **Is** (**Are**) there any students from China in your class?

   B: Yes, there **is**   **are**   five students from China. **They**   **There**   are from Beijing.

2. A: Is there **an**   **any**   elevator in this building?

   B: Yes, **there**   **it**   is. **There**   **It**   is at the end of the hall.

3. A: **Is**   **Are**   there a ladies' room on this floor?

   B: No, there **isn't**   **aren't**.   **There**   **It**   is one on the second floor.

4. A: Are there any vending   **machine**   machines   on this floor?

   B: Yes,   **they**   there   are.   **There**   They   are in the student lounge.

5. A: Is there a copy   machine   **machines**   for student use?

   B: Yes,   **there**   it   is one in the library. It costs ten cents a copy.

6. A: Are there many   computer   **computers**   in the library?

   B: Yes, there are   one   **a lot of**   computers in the library.

7. A: Is   **Are**   there a fax machine in the library?

   B: No, there   isn't   **aren't.** There is   **a**   some   fax machine in the student center.

◼ C. LEGAL HOLIDAYS

Holidays	
New Year's Day	January 1st
Martin Luther King Day	January 15th
President's Day	The third Monday in February
Memorial Day	The last Monday in May
Independence Day	July 4th
Labor Day	The first Monday in September
Columbus Day	Second Monday in October
Election Day	The first Tuesday after the first Monday in November
Thanksgiving	The fourth Thursday in November
Christmas	December 25th

Use the information about legal holidays. Put the questions in order and then write the answer to each question.

1. legal / How many / there / every / holidays / are / year ?

   How many legal holidays are there every year   ?

   _____ .

2. January 1st / there / on / Are / any / classes ?

_____ ?

_____ .

3. there / November / How many / in / are / holidays ?

_____ ?

_____ .

4. September / are / holidays / How many / in / there ?

_____ ?

_____ .

5. in / there / Are / March / holidays / any ?

_____ ?

_____ .

6. Thanksgiving / classes / there / on / Are / any ?

_____ ?

_____ .

7. many / Are / in / holidays / there / country / your?

_____ ?

_____ .

Having Fun with the Language

■ **A. A BLUEPRINT** *Work in groups of three or four students. Go to different rooms or areas in your school building, for example, the cafeteria, library, lobby, main floor, lounge, etc. Draw a detailed blueprint of the area. Only include large items in your drawing, such as desks, tables, bookshelves, and other furniture.*

 Then, write ten sentences about the room. Come back to class and draw your blueprint on the blackboard or a large piece of paper. Read your description to your classmates.

■ B. IMPORTANT NUMBERS
How many are there? Can you match the numbers on the left and the information on the right? The answers are on page 113.

10   There are ___50___ states in the United States.

3   There are _____ countries in North America.

4   There are _____ provinces in Canada.

5   There are _____ continental states on the Pacific Ocean.*

4   There are _____ states that start with the word **New.**

3   There are _____ states on the Gulf of Mexico.

5   There are _____ states not within the continental U.S.

50   There are _____ states that border on Mexico.

4   There are _____ time zones in the continental United States.

2   There are _____ Great Lakes.

   * continental: all states except Hawaii and Alaska

■ C. SPORTS
How many players are there on each of these teams? The answers are on page 113.

_____ ice hockey

_____ volleyball

_____ football

_____ baseball

_____ soccer

_____ basketball

Grammar Summary

I. Statements

There	is	a	student	in the classroom.
			computer	
			desk	
	are	a few	students	
		several	computers	
		a lot of	desks	

2. Affirmative

There is a computer in the classroom.

There are some computers in the classroom.

Negative

There **isn't a** computer in the classroom.

There **is no** computer in the classroom.

There **aren't any** computers in the classroom.

There **are no** computers in the classroom.

3. *How many questions*

How many students are there in the classroom?	There are twenty.
How many clocks are there in the classroom?	There is one.
How many computers are there in the classroom?	There aren't any.

4. Quantity words *We sometimes use a quantifier instead of an exact number.*

a few	several	some
many	a lot of (lots of)	

Unit 12: Answers for Having Fun with the Language

B. IMPORTANT NUMBERS

There are 50 states in the United States.

There are 3 countries in North America.

There are 10 provinces in Canada.

There are 3 continental states on the Pacific Ocean.

There are 4 states that start with the word *New.*

There are 5 states on the Gulf of Mexico.

There are 2 states not within the continental U.S.

There are 4 states that border on Mexico.

There are 4 time zones in the continental United States.

There are 5 Great Lakes.

C. SPORTS

6	ice hockey	6	volleyball	11	football
9	baseball	11	soccer	5	basketball

Weather

Can

Grammar in Action

■ **A. WEATHER** *Repeat these sentences after your teacher. Ask about any new words.*

It's sunny.   It's raining.   It's snowing.
It's cloudy.   It's windy.   It's foggy.

Write the weather under each picture.

1. _____

2. _____

3. _____

4. _____

5. _____

6. _____

■ B. THE TEMPERATURE Look at the thermometers and give the temperature.

EXAMPLE

It's cool. It's 50°.

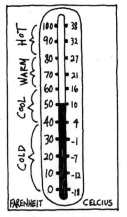
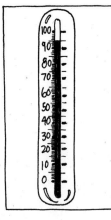
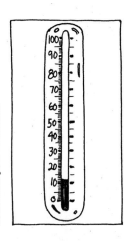
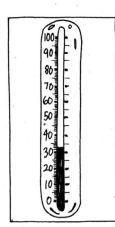
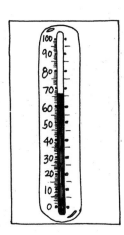

C. LISTEN: A WEATHER REPORT Listen to the weather report. Put the correct picture and temperature for each city on the map.

sunny

cloudy

raining

windy

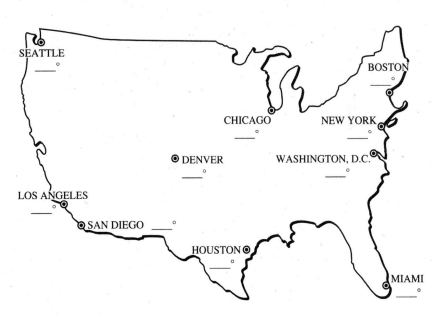

■ D. QUESTIONS Answer these questions about the weather map.

1. Is it sunny in Miami? What's the temperature there?
2. What's the weather in Boston? Is it cold in Boston today?
3. Is it raining in Denver? What's the temperature there?
4. What's the weather in Los Angeles? Is it sunny there today?
5. Is it hot or cold in Chicago today? What's the weather in Chicago today?
6. What area of the country do you live in? What's the weather today? What's the temperature?
7. Which area of the United States has the kind of weather that you like?

▪ E. THE SEASONS *Talk about the seasons in your area of the country.*

Winter	Spring	Summer	Fall
Dec. 21–March 21	March 21–June 21	June 21–Sept. 21	Sept. 21–Dec. 21

What season is it in each picture?

What are the people doing? What are they wearing?

How many seasons do you have in your area of the United States or Canada?

What's the weather in each season? What season is it now?

What's your favorite season? Why?

■ A. SPORTS Repeat each sport after your teacher. Ask about any new words. Which sports are in the illustrations?

ski	ice skate	swim
skateboard	surf	roller blade
play baseball	play tennis	play soccer
ride a bicycle	sail	lift weights

 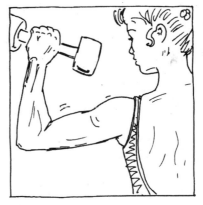

■ B. QUESTIONS Answer these questions about sports and activities.

EXAMPLE

Can you ski?	**Can she ski?**	**Can he ski?**
Yes, I can.	Yes, she can.	Yes, he can.
No, I can't.	No, she can't.	No, he can't.

1. Can you ski?
2. Can your teacher ski?
3. Can you ice skate?
4. Can you ride a bicycle?
5. Can you run a mile?

6. Can you roller blade?
7. Can you play tennis?
8. Can your teacher play tennis?
9. Can you sail?
10. Can you swim?

C. LISTEN: CAN OR CAN'T *Listen and circle the word you hear.*

PRONUNCIATION

can   I can swim.   I can ice skate.

can't   I can't swim.   I can't ice skate.

1. I (can) can't   play tennis.
2. She   can   can't   run a mile.
3. My brother   can   can't   surf.
4. I   can   can't   ice skate.
5. I   can   can't   play baseball.
6. My father   can   can't   sail.
7. You   can   can't   ski well.
8. I   can   can't   play soccer.
9. I   can   can't   ride a bicycle.
10. My sister   can   can't   roller blade.

Working Together

A. INTERVIEW *If possible, sit with a student from a different continent. Ask your partner to show you his / her country on a map. Ask these questions and complete the information in the chart.*

Questions	Partner
1. What country are you from?	
2. How many seasons are there in your country?	
3. Do you have a rainy season?	
4. Does it snow a lot in your country?	
5. How's the weather in June?	
6. How's the weather in January?	
7. How's the weather in your country now?	

B. SPORTS IN YOUR AREA *Talk about the seasons and outside activities in your area of the United States or Canada.*

> **EXAMPLE**
>
> You can ski in Canada in the winter. It snows a lot.
> You can go to Mt. Tremblant or Whistler.
>
> It's really hot here in Florida. You can swim or sail or spend all day in the water. You can't play tennis or ride a bicycle in the middle of the day. In the summer, it's too hot.

D. STUDENT TO STUDENT

Student A: *Circle the information that is true for you (1 to 7). Read your sentences to* **Student B.** *Do not look at each other's books!*

Student B: *Listen to* **Student A.** *Circle his or her answers.*

Student A

1. I **can** **can't** swim.

2. I **can** **can't** play tennis.

3. I **can** **can't** roller blade.

4. I **can** **can't** lift weights.

5. I **can** **can't** ski.

6. I **can** **can't** run a mile.

7. I **can** **can't** ride a bicycle.

Student B

8. I **can** **can't** swim.

9. I **can** **can't** play tennis.

10. I **can** **can't** roller blade.

11. I **can** **can't** lift weights.

12. I **can** **can't** ski.

13. I **can** **can't** run a mile.

14. I **can** **can't** ride a bicycle.

When you finish, **Student B** *will then circle and read his or her information (8 to 14).* **Student A** *will listen and circle the answers.*

◼ A. THE WEATHER MAP *Answer these questions about the weather map.*

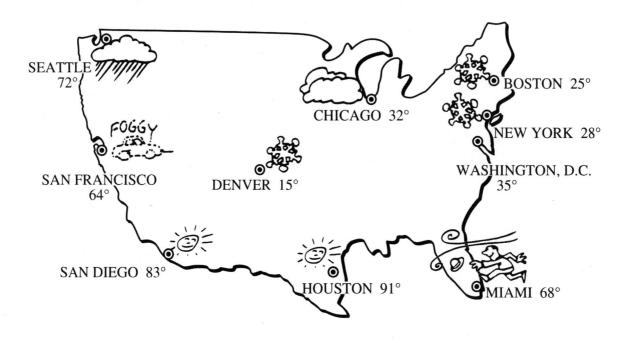

1. What's the weather in New York City? _____

2. Is it cold there today? _____

3. What's the temperature in Houston? _____

4. Is it raining there? _____

5. What's the weather in Seattle? _____

6. What's the temperature there? _____

7. Is it snowing in Boston? _____

8. What's the temperature there? _____

9. What's the weather in San Diego? _____

10. Is it windy in San Diego? _____

■ B. QUESTIONS *Write questions about the weather map on page 128.*

1. _____ in New York?   It's snowing.

2. _____ ?   Yes, it is.

3. _____ in Denver?   It's 15°.

4. _____ ?   It's snowing.

5. _____ in Boston?   No, it isn't.

6. _____ in Boston?   It's 25°.

7. _____ in Miami?   It's 68°.

8. _____ ?   It's cloudy?

9. _____ in San Francisco?   It's foggy.

10. _____ ?   No, it isn't.

■ C. TODAY'S WEATHER *Answer these questions about the weather in your area.*

1. What state or province do you live in?   _____

2. What season is it?   _____

3. What's the weather today?   _____

4. What's the temperature?   _____

5. Is it sunny?   _____

6. Is it windy?   _____

7. Is this typical weather for your area?   _____

8. What can you do outside today?   _____

Having Fun with the Language

A. FIND SOMEONE WHO *Stand up and walk around the classroom. Ask several students about the activities below. Think of two new sports or activities. Try to find someone for each activity and write that student's name.*

EXAMPLE

Can you dance?   No, I can't. *(Keep asking!)*

Can you dance?   Yes, I can. *(Write that student's name)*

1. Can you dance? _____

2. Can you cook Italian food? _____

3. Can you play the guitar? _____

4. Can you lift 100 pounds? _____

5. Can you sail a boat? _____

6. Can you ice skate backwards? _____

7. Can you run five miles? _____

8. Can you play the piano? _____

9. Can you _____? _____

10. Can you _____? _____

B. THE WEATHER REPORT *Your teacher will record the weather report from the radio and play it in class. Listen for words you know. What is the temperature? What is the forecast for tomorrow?*

Look in the newspaper for the weather map. Bring it to class and discuss the weather for today and tomorrow.

You are a weather forecaster; write the weather report for a "perfect day."

Grammar Summary

■ 1. Weather

What's the weather in Chicago?   It's cold and windy.

What's the temperature?   It's 38°.

■ 2. *Can* statements

I You He She We They	can can't	ski. swim. roller blade.

■ 3. *Yes/no* questions

Can	I you he she we they	ski? swim?

. . . . Yes, you can.   No, you can't.
. . . . Yes, I can.   No, I can't.
. . . . Yes, he can.   No, he can't.
. . . . Yes, she can.   No, she can't.
. . . . Yes, you can.   No, you can't.
. . . . Yes, they can.   No, they can't.

Surf City

Past Tense of *Be*

A. ADJECTIVES *Repeat these words after your teacher. Ask about any new words. Are any of these words opposites?*

dirty	small	comfortable	terrible
large	clean	friendly	quiet
old	happy	noisy	uncomfortable
upset	new	wonderful	unfriendly

124

B. LISTEN: A SHORT VACATION
On Labor Day weekend, Michael and Patty took a short vacation. On Saturday they stayed in Bayside and had a terrible day. On Sunday, they stayed in Surf City and had a wonderful time. Listen to their story.

C. LISTEN: A WEEKEND VACATION
Listen to each sentence and circle the beach that it describes.

1. (Bayside)   Surf City   6. Bayside   Surf City

2. Bayside   Surf City   7. Bayside   Surf City

3. Bayside   Surf City   8. Bayside   Surf City

4. Bayside   Surf City   9. Bayside   Surf City

5. Bayside   Surf City   10. Bayside   Surf City

■ D. A BAD VACATION AND A GOOD VACATION
Each sentence tells about the day in Bayside. Read the description, and then tell about the day in Surf City.

EXAMPLE

In Bayside, the beach was dirty.   In Surf City, the beach was clean.

1. In Bayside, the weather was cloudy.
2. In Bayside, the temperature was cool.
3. In Bayside, the beach was dirty.
4. In Bayside, the water was dirty.
5. In Bayside, the motel was old.
6. In Bayside, the motel was noisy.
7. In Bayside, the bed was uncomfortable.
8. In Bayside, the towels were dirty.
9. In Bayside, the room was small.
10. In Bayside, everything was terrible.

■ E. *HOW* QUESTIONS
Ask and answer questions about Michael and Patty's vacation.

EXAMPLE

How was the weather in Bayside?   It was cloudy and cool.

How	was	the weather the motel the room the beach	in Bayside? in Surf City?

▪ A. A GOOD RESTAURANT

Complete this chart about a restaurant you like in your city (not a fast food restaurant). Then, tell a partner about the restaurant. If possible, sit with a person who likes the same restaurant as you and compare your responses.

Question	Response
1. What is the name of a restaurant you like?	
2. Where is it?	
3. When was the last time you ate there?	
4. What was the occasion?	
5. How was the service?	
6. How was the food?	
7. Was the restaurant noisy?	
8. Were the waiters or waitresses friendly?	
9. Was it expensive?	

▪ B. A RESTAURANT REVIEW

Complete this review of the restaurant you wrote about in Exercise A.

Name of restaurant: _____

Type of food: _____

Location: _____

Service: ☐ excellent ☐ good ☐ poor

Atmosphere: ☐ noisy ☐ quiet ☐ romantic ☐ crowded

Food: ☐ delicious ☐ good ☐ fair ☐ terrible

Price range: ☐ expensive ☐ moderate ☐ inexpensive

Recommended dishes: _____

Tell your class or another group about the restaurant you reviewed.

C. LET'S EAT OUT

Americans eat out about six times a month. What are their favorite kinds of ethnic food? Talk about the chart with these sentences. There are many possible answers.

Favorite Ethnic Foods	
Italian	36%
Chinese	23%
Mexican	20%
French	8%
German	6%
Greek	2%
Japanese	2%
Other	3%

1. The favorite kind of ethnic food is _____ .

2. Americans enjoy _____ food more than _____ food.

3. _____ % of people like _____ food.

4. My favorite kind of ethnic food is _____ .

5. I have never tried _____ food.

6. I would like to try _____ food.

7. I don't like _____ food.

Survey the students in your class. Each student can choose his or her favorite kind of ethnic food. Make a chart to show the choices.

Sharing Our Stories

Read Huasong's story about the Wok Inn. Then write a description of a restaurant you like. Write about what you ordered, how much it cost, the service and the atmosphere.

Last month, my wife and I ate at the Wok Inn, a Chinese restaurant. We arrived at 7:00 and we had to wait for a table for twenty minutes. The menu was long. We ordered shrimp with vegetables and chicken with hot sauce. The service was very fast. The waiter brought our order in just ten minutes. We liked the shrimp with vegetables because it was fresh and delicious. The chicken with hot sauce was too spicy. The restaurant was noisy. The Wok Inn is good for families because it is not too expensive. Our dinner was $23.

Huasong Lee

A. COMPLETE *On their vacation, Patty and Michael ate at two different restaurants. They had a terrible time at Café de Paris. Everything was wrong. They had a wonderful evening at La Casita. Everything was perfect. Complete these sentences about the two restaurants with* **was, wasn't, were,** *or* **weren't.**

1. In Café de Paris, the food _____was_____ terrible.

2. The meal _____ cold and the food _____ fresh.

3. In La Casita, the food _____ delicious.

4. The food _____ spicy, but it _____ too spicy.

5. In Café de Paris, the service _____ slow. The waiters _____ friendly.

6. In La Casita, the service _____ good and the waiters _____ friendly.

7. In Café de Paris, Patty and Michael's table _____ near the kitchen.

8. In La Casita, their table _____ near the window.

9. In Café de Paris, their table _____ small and the chairs _____ comfortable.

   They _____ happy to leave!

10. In La Casita, Patty and Michael _____ happy and satisfied.

B. YES / NO QUESTIONS *Use the chart and write seven questions and answers about the restaurants.*

In Cafe de Paris,	was	the food the service the dinner	delicious? slow? spicy?
In La Casita,	were	the waiters Michael and Patty	friendly? helpful? happy? expensive?

ANSWERS

Yes, it was.   Yes, they were.

No, it wasn't.   No, they weren't.

1. In Café de Paris, was the food spicy _____?

   No, it wasn't _____.

2. _____?

   _____.

3. _____?

   _____.

4. _____?

   _____.

5. _____?

   _____.

6. _____?

   _____.

7. _____?

   _____.

■ C. WRITE THE QUESTIONS *Read the story. Then, complete the questions.*

It was Labor Day and Michael and Patty decided to go away for the last weekend of the summer.

On Saturday, they drove to Bayside. Everything was terrible! The weather was cloudy and cool. The beaches were dirty with cups, cans, and bottles on the sand. Because their motel was near the highway, it was very noisy and they were awake most of the night. On Saturday evening, they tried a French restaurant near their motel. Their table was near the kitchen and it was hot and noisy. The food was awful. Patty said, "I can cook better than this!" Michael was upset with the bill. It was $75.

Patty and Michael left on Sunday morning and drove to Surf City. What a difference! The weather was sunny and hot. The beach was sandy and white, and they were in the water all afternoon. Their motel was on a quiet street near the beach. That evening, they were happy with the Mexican restaurant near the motel. Their table was near the window, so they could see the beach. The food was fresh and spicy, and the bill was only $37.

1. How was the weather in Bayside ?   It was cloudy and cool.

2. Why _____ ?   Because it was near the highway.

3. Where _____ ?   It was near the kitchen.

4. How _____ ?   It was awful.

5. How much _____ ?   It was $75.

6. How _____ ?   It was sunny and hot.

7. Where _____ ?   In the water.

8. Where _____ ?   Near the motel.

9. How _____ ?   Fresh and spicy.

10. How much _____ ?   It was $37.

Having Fun with the Language

■ A. WHO WAS THE FIRST . . . ? *Match these questions and answers. Check your answers on page 131.*

1. Who was the first person to walk on the moon?   a. Valentina Tereshkova
2. Who was the first woman in space?   b. Charles Lindbergh
3. Who was the first person to fly from New York to Paris?   c. George Washington
4. Who was the first female president of a country?   d. Neil Armstrong
5. Who was the first woman to serve on the Supreme Court?   e. Richard Nixon
6. Who was the first woman to fly from New York to Paris?   f. Ferdinand Magellan
7. Who was the first president of the United States?   g. Sandra Day O'Connor
8. Who was the first person to orbit the earth?   h. Amelia Earhardt
9. Who was the first president to resign?   i. Yuri Gagarin
10. Who was the first person to sail around the world?   j. Isabel Perón

Work with a small group. Use a World Almanac, history text, or information you know. Prepare five questions beginning with phrases such as:

Who was the first...

Who was the youngest

Ask your questions to the class.

1. Statements

I He She It	was	quiet. hot.
We You They	were	clean

2. Yes/no questions

Was	I he she it	hot?
Were	we you they	

. . .Yes, you were.   No, you weren't.
. . .Yes, he was.   No, he wasn't.
. . .Yes, she was.   No, she wasn't.
. . .Yes, it was.   No, it wasn't.
. . .Yes, you were.   No, you weren't.
. . .Yes, we were.   No, we weren't.
. . .Yes, they were. No, they weren't.

3. Wh questions

How was the motel?   . . .   It was comfortable.
Where was the motel?   . . .   In Bayside.
How were the waiters?   . . .   They were friendly.

Unit 12: Answers for Having Fun with the Language

A.   1. d   2. a   3. b   4. j   5. g

         6. h   7. c   8. i   9. e   10. f

Last Weekend

Past Tense

Grammar in Action

A. PAST VERBS *Repeat these past verbs after your teacher. Ask about any new words.*

Regular Past Verbs

applied	picked up
deposited	stopped at
dropped off	talked
looked at	tried on
mailed	waited
ordered	walked

Irregular Past Verbs

be–was, were	have–had
buy–bought	leave–left
feel–felt	pay–paid
find–found	read–read
get–got	spend–spent
go–went	take–took

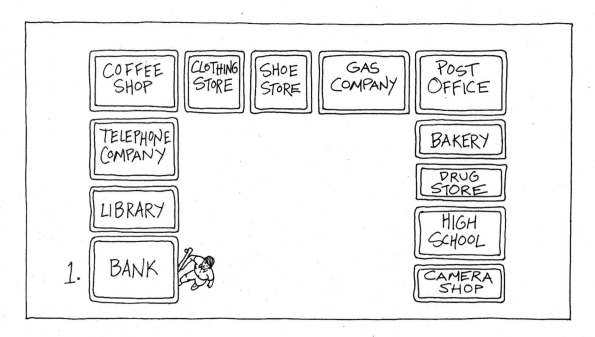

B. LISTEN: ALI'S MORNING

Ali went downtown on Saturday morning. Listen to the tape. Where did he go first, second, third, etc? Number the locations from 1 to 7 on the map on page 132.

■ C. TALK ABOUT THE STORY

Complete this information about Ali's morning downtown.

1. Ali went downtown last _____Saturday_____ .

2. First, he went to the _____ .

3. He tried on _____ at the shoe store.

4. Then he stopped at the _____ .

5. He waited in line for _____ minutes.

6. At the post office he bought some _____ .

7. At the coffee shop he ordered juice, _____ , and _____ .

8. At the library he read the _____ .

9. At the camera store he picked up _____ from his son's birthday party.

10. He _____ home.

D. LISTEN FOR AMOUNTS

Listen again and complete these sentences with the correct amount.

1. Ali took $ _____ out of the bank.

2. He paid $ _____ at the gas company.

3. He spent $ _____ at the coffee shop, $ _____ at the post office, and

   $ _____ at the camera store.

4. He had $ _____ left when he went home.

E. LISTEN: PAST TENSE VERBS *Listen and fill in the past tense verb.*

1. I ____walked____ downtown.

2. I _____ my paycheck in the bank.

3. I _____ $100 in cash.

4. I _____ on some sneakers.

5. I _____ anything.

6. There _____ a lot of people in line.

7. I _____ in line fifteen minutes.

8. I _____ a letter to my brother.

9. I _____ $10 at the post office.

10. I _____ at the coffee shop.

11. I _____ a cup of coffee.

12. The bill _____ $2.50.

13. I _____ a fifty-cent tip.

14. I _____ out a book on car repairs.

15. I _____ up my pictures.

16. I _____ at the drugstore.

Regular Past Tense Verbs

■ A. LISTEN: -ED

Final -ed is pronounced as /d/ or /t/ after most verbs. Do not add a syllable to the verb.

EXAMPLE

play	played	walk	walked
mail	mailed	stop	stopped
try	tried	look	looked

Final -ed is pronounced as /ɪd/ after t and d. Add a syllable to the verb.

EXAMPLE

| need | needed |
| wait | waited |

Underline the verb in each sentence. Then, listen to each sentence on the tape. Write the number of syllables you hear in each verb. Read the sentences to a partner.

EXAMPLE

___1___ Ali _walked_ downtown.

___2___ He _needed_ a pair of sneakers.

1. ____ Ali walked to the bank.
2. ____ He wanted a pair of sneakers.
3. ____ Ali stopped at the gas company.
4. ____ He waited in line for 15 minutes.
5. ____ He talked to some of the people in line.
6. ____ Ali needed some stamps.
7. ____ Ali mailed a letter to his brother.
8. ____ He looked at the newspaper from his country.
9. ____ Ali picked up some pictures.
10. ____ He started home again.

B. SPELLING

Look at the spelling rules on pages 144–145. Write each verb in the past tense. Then, write the number of syllables in each verb.

clean	cleaned (1)	study	_____
call	_____	wash	_____
rent	_____	stop	_____
prepare	_____	visit	_____
finish	_____	play	_____
watch	_____	stay	_____

C. LAURA'S DAY

Laura was busy last Saturday. Read about her day and fill in the verbs in the past tense. Then, read the story to a partner. Pay attention to the pronunciation of -ed.

Saturday is Laura's favorite day. She doesn't have to go to work or to school. Last Saturday morning, Laura went to the park and _____ (play) tennis for two hours with one of her friends. On the way home, she _____ (stop) at the deli and _____ (pick) up a sandwich for lunch. In the afternoon, Laura _____ (clean) her apartment and she _____ (wash) her clothes at the laundromat. In the evening, Laura _____ (visit) her sister and brother-in-law in the next town. Her sister _____ (prepare) a few salads and her brother-in-law _____ (cook) chicken on the grill. They _____ (talk) about politics, jobs, and their families. Laura _____ (stay) until midnight. When she got home, she _____ (call) her family in Italy.

D. LAST WEEKEND

D. LAST WEEKEND *What did you do last weekend? Check the sentences that are true and read them to a partner.*

1. ☐ I cleaned my house.   ☐ I didn't clean my home.

2. ☐ I washed my clothes.   ☐ I didn't wash my clothes.

3. ☐ I worked.   ☐ I didn't work.

4. ☐ I watched a movie.   ☐ I didn't watch a movie.

5. ☐ I studied.   ☐ I didn't study.

6. ☐ I visited friends.   ☐ I didn't visit friends.

7. ☐ I called my family.   ☐ I didn't call my family.

Write two more things you did last weekend.

1. _____

2. _____

Write two more things you didn't do last weekend.

1. _____

2. _____

Irregular Past Tense Verbs

A. IRREGULAR PAST *Study the irregular past verbs on page 176. Write the past tense of these verbs.*

pay _____	have _____
go _____	take _____
buy _____	get _____
drink _____	drive _____
be _____	say _____
find _____	sit _____
eat _____	leave _____
feel _____	spend _____

■ B. A DAY IN THE CITY

Read about Kate and David's day in the city. Underline the regular past tense verbs. Circle the irregular past tense verbs.

Last Sunday, Kate and David (drove) into the city. It was Sunday, so the traffic was light. It only took them about 45 minutes. They paid ten dollars to park in a parking lot in the center of the city. Then, they walked to the art museum. They had tickets, but they had to stand in line for almost an hour to get in. The museum had a special exhibit, the World of Picasso, so the museum was busy. Kate and David looked at the exhibit for about two hours. Then, they went to the gift shop. Kate bought a poster and Jack got a book of Picasso's most famous paintings. They both felt tired, so they found a nice coffee shop across from the museum. They sat for an hour and drank espresso and talked. David said, "Let's come into the city more often. We really had a great day!"

■ C. CORRECT IT!

This information about the story above is not correct. Find the mistakes. Use a negative, and then say the sentence correctly.

> **EXAMPLE**
>
> Kate and David paid <u>twenty dollars</u> to park.
>
> They <u>didn't pay twenty dollars</u> to park.
>
> They paid <u>ten</u> dollars.

1. They went to the Science Museum.

2. It took one hour to drive into the city.

3. The museum had an exhibit of paintings by Van Gogh.

4. Jack bought some note cards.

5. They found a nice deli near the museum.

6. They drank wine.

7. They had a terrible day.

◼ D. PAST TIME EXPRESSIONS *Study these past time expressions, then use them with the words below.*

last	ago	yesterday
last night	ten minutes ago	yesterday
last Sunday	an hour ago	yesterday morning
last weekend	three days ago	yesterday afternoon
last week	a week ago	yesterday evening
last month	a month ago	
last year	a year ago	

EXAMPLE

I went to an art museum last year.

went to an art museum	took a walk	went downtown
paid my telephone bill	did my homework	saw a good movie
began to study English	read the newspaper	ate out

Working Together

◼ A. MY WEEKEND *Where did you go last weekend? Check the places you went. Then, tell your partner about each place and what you did there.*

☐ the bank	☐ the laundromat	☐ the drugstore	☐ the supermarket
☐ the post office	☐ church	☐ school	☐ my friend's house
☐ the library	☐ work	☐ the barber shop	☐ _____
☐ the park	☐ the mall	☐ a restaurant	☐ _____

EXAMPLE

I went to the supermarket. I bought milk, eggs, and chicken.

My husband and I went to the laundromat. We washed our clothes.

◼ B. INTERVIEW *Ask your partner about last weekend. If your partner's answer is **Yes,** check the day on the chart.*

EXAMPLE

Did you sleep late?   Did you sleep late?

No, I didn't.   Yes, I slept late on Sunday.

Activity	Saturday	Sunday
Did you sleep late?		
Did you go to the supermarket?		
Did you do the laundry?		
Did you clean your house or apartment?		
Did you work?		
Did you do your homework?		
Did you call a relative?		
Did you watch TV?		
Did you exercise?		
Did you go shopping?		
Did you eat out?		
Did you cook?		
Did you visit friends?		

■ C. REPORT INFORMATION FROM THE CHART *Look at the chart and complete this information about your partner. Write the day in the blank.*

1. My partner   **slept   didn't sleep**   late on _____.

2. My partner   **got up   didn't get up**   early on _____.

3. My partner   **went   didn't go**   to the supermarket this weekend.

4. My partner   **worked   didn't work**   this weekend.

5. My partner   **called   didn't call**   a relative this weekend.

Complete these sentences about your partner. Write the day in the second blank.

6. My partner _____ TV on _____.

7. My partner _____ this weekend.

8. My partner _____ shopping this weekend.

9. My partner _____ a big dinner on _____.

10. My partner _____ friends on _____.

C. STUDENT TO STUDENT

Student A: *Turn to page 186. Read the seven sentences to* **Student B.**

Student B: *Listen to the information. If the sentence is true, write about yourself. If the sentence isn't true, write the negative.*

A: You got up late.

B: (Write) I got up late. or I didn't get up late.

1. _____

2. _____

3. _____

4. _____

5. _____

6. _____

7. _____

When you finish, **Student B** will turn to page 186 and read seven new sentences to **Student A.**

Practicing on Your Own

■ A. PAST TENSE *Complete this story with the past tense of the verbs.*

Last Saturday night, I _____went_____ (go) out with my wife. We

_____ (do) our chores in the morning. We _____

(clean) our house and _____ (go) food shopping at the supermarket.

Then, we _____ (visit) my wife's parents, and at around 5:00 p.m. we

_____ (be) free, so we _____ (decide) to go to a

restaurant for dinner at 7:00 p.m. We _____ (eat) at Faroles

Restaurant and we _____ (have) Spanish food.

It _____ (be) a little uncomfortable for us in the restaurant because we _____ (have) to take our daughter with us. Betty, our daughter, is twenty months old. She's very noisy. She walked around or _____ (sit) under the table the whole time. She _____ (say) "Hi!" to everyone. Anyway, we _____ (enjoy) the dinner because we _____ (be) together.

After we _____ (finish) dinner, we _____ (drive) to the park. We _____ (put) our daughter in the stroller and _____ (walk) around the lake. It _____ (be) so beautiful and so quiet. My daughter _____ (fall) asleep in her stroller.

We go out almost every Saturday. Sometimes we go to a restaurant, a movie, or to a party. We think it's good to relax after a hard week's work!

Cesar Vargas, Peru

■ B. NEGATIVES *Complete these sentences about the story in Exercise A. Write the verb in the negative.*

1. They _____ out on Friday night; they went out on Saturday night.

2. They _____ their chores on Saturday evening; they did their chores on Saturday morning.

3. They _____ his wife's sister; they visited his wife's parents.

4. They _____ free in the morning; they were free in the evening.

5. They _____ in an Italian restaurant; they ate at a Spanish restaurant.

6. Their daughter _____ in a chair; she sat under the table.

7. They didn't _____ to the park; they drove to the park.

8. The park _____ noisy; it was quiet.

9. Their daughter _____ asleep in the car; she fell asleep in her stroller.

10. They _____ home late; they got home early.

Rosa wrote a story about her day on Sunday. Read her story, and then write about your weekend. Use the past tense.

We had a long, cold winter and it's finally spring. Yesterday it was sunny and warm. I decided to celebrate. We have a small balcony on our apartment. I cleaned the floor. Then I went to our storage area in the basement and found the two outdoor chairs. My husband, Hugo, carried them upstairs. I love flowers, so I drove to the florist and bought two hanging flower baskets. We hung them up and my husband and I sat out in the sun. We talked and watched the activity in the street and enjoyed the warm weather.

Rosa Aguilar

■ A. PLAYING WITH THE IRREGULAR PAST
Study the irregular past verbs on page 176. Then have an irregular past bee, similar to a spelling bee. Ten students stand in front of the room. Your teacher says a verb in the simple form, and the first student says the verb in the past. The teacher continues in order, giving one verb to each student, then beginning again with the first student. If a student makes a mistake, he/she has to sit down.

■ B. YOU'RE LYING!
A student comes up to the front of the classroom and makes three statements about last weekend. Two sentences are true and one sentence is false. The other students try to guess which statement is false.

EXAMPLE

Student: I bought a TV set. I called my sister in Colombia. I found $5 on the sidewalk.

Guesses: I think you bought a TV set.
I think you called your sister is Colombia.
I think you're lying. You didn't find $5 on the sidewalk.

Student: Yes, I did! I found $5 on the sidewalk. I didn't buy a TV.

■ C. ORDERING
Your teacher will give each student eight small cards or pieces of paper. On each, write down one thing you did yesterday. You do not have to write a complete sentence, you can write: **soccer, lunch with my friends, a gift for my brother,** *etc. Then, sit with a partner and describe your day in detail. Your partner has to listen and place the cards in order.*

Grammar Summary

■ I. Past tense
Use the simple past tense to talk about things you did in the past (yesterday, last week, etc.).

Regular past verbs end with **ed.**

The chart of irregular past verbs is on page 176 in the appendix.

◼ 2. Statements

I We You They He She It	cooked enjoyed prepared ate made	dinner.

3. Negatives

I We You They He She It	didn't did not	cook enjoy prepare eat make	dinner.

◼ 4. *Yes/no questions*

Did I **finish?**	. . . Yes, you did.	No, you didn't.
Did you **get** up early?	. . . Yes, I did.	No, I didn't.
Did he **work** yesterday?	. . . Yes, he did.	No, he didn't.
Did she **do** her homework?	. . . Yes, she did.	No, she didn't.
Did it **rain?**	. . . Yes, it did.	No, it didn't.
Did we **study** this?	. . . Yes, you did.	No, you didn't.
Did you **buy** your books?	. . . Yes, we did.	No, we didn't.
Did they **paint** their house?	. . . Yes, they did.	No, they didn't.

◼ 5. Spelling

Verb Ending		Spelling
1. Most verbs	→	Add **ed**
open mail walk		open**ed** mail**ed** walk**ed**
2. Verbs that end with **e**	→	Add **d**
smil**e** arriv**e**		smiled arrived

3. Verbs that end with a consonant, vowel, consonant $\rightarrow$	Double the final consonant
st**op**	stop**ped**
rob	rob**bed**

* Do not double a final **w, x,** or **y**

fix	fix**ed**
play	play**ed**

4. Verbs that end with a consonant and **y** $\rightarrow$	Change the **y** to **i**, add **ed**
tr**y**	tr**ied**
stu**dy**	stud**ied**

Growing Up

Past Tense Questions

Grammar in Action

■ A. VOCABULARY *Repeat these verbs after your teacher. Ask about any new words.*

Regular Past Verbs

graduated   moved

learned   played

lived   started

Irregular Past Verbs

be–was, were   know–knew

break–broke   make–made

fall–fell   teach–taught

get–got   win–won

■ B. LISTEN: OSCAR *Listen to Oscar talk about his life. The second time you listen, write one past tense verb under each picture. Retell his story.*

■ C. ASK AND ANSWER *Ask and answer these questions with **Did.***

> **EXAMPLE**
>
> **Did Oscar break his arm?**   **Did you break your arm?**
>
> Yes, he did.   Yes, I did.
>
> No, he didn't   No, I didn't.

Did	Oscar / you	break his / your arm?
		have the chicken pox?
		move to the United States alone?
		go to high school in the United States?
		play a sport in high school?
		fall in love in high school?
		graduate from high school?
		work while in high school?

■ D. PAST TENSE QUESTIONS *Answer these questions about Oscar's life.*

1. Where was Oscar born? When did he start school?

2. How did he break his arm?

3. When did he get the chicken pox? Who else got chicken pox?

4. What sport did he play in school?   Was he a good player?

5. When did he move to the United States? What state did he move to?

6. Who lived there first?

7. Where did he go to high school?

8. Why didn't he like the United States at first?

9. Who taught him how to drive?

10. Where did he find a job?

11. When did he start college?

When I came to the United States three years ago, I didn't know how to drive. Bus service in Lincoln wasn't good, so I needed to drive to get to my job at the hospital. My brother taught me how to drive. Every weekend he took me to the high school parking lot. I practiced going straight, backing up, turning, stopping, and parking. I only practiced in the parking lot. Eight weeks later, I took the driving test at the Department of Motor Vehicles. Unfortunately, I was very nervous and I made a lot of mistakes. I forgot to signal when I turned, I didn't stop at the stop signs, and I didn't park correctly. I failed the test. After that, I practiced in my neighborhood and around town. Four weeks later, I passed the test.

Molly Lim, Singapore

1. When did Molly come to the United States?

2. Was the bus service good in her town?

3. Why did she need to drive?

4. Who taught her?

5. When did they practice?

6. Where did she practice?

7. What did she practice?

8. Where did she take the test?

9. Why did she fail the test?

10. When did she pass the test?

Read Aileen's story about her graduation day.

    I will never forget the day of my graduation from high school. Graduation was in the evening. At 5:30, my friends and I arrived at school. All my classmates were in the auditorium. We put on our caps and gowns and got in line. Then, at 6:30 the class marched outside to the football field where they held the ceremony. The school band played and our families cheered and clapped as we marched onto the field. We approached our chairs, everyone sat down, and we listened to speeches by the superintendent and the principal. Then we all received our diplomas. Finally, the graduation ceremony was over and we all cried and hugged. Our parents took lots of photographs.

    After the graduation, my parents took me out to dinner at a restaurant. When dinner was over, we drove home. I was surprised to see a lot of cars in my street. I thought that one of my neighbors was having a party. To my surprise, when I walked into the house, my relatives and friends were at the door shouting "Congratulations!" I was so happy. I could not believe that my parents were giving me a surprise party!

Aileen Tolentino, The Philippines

Write the questions for these answers.

1. __When was Aileen's graduation?_____ In the evening.

2. _____ At 5:30.

3. _____ Their caps and gowns.

4. _____ To the football field.

5. _____ Their diplomas.

6. _____ They cried and hugged.

7. _____ Their parents.

8. _____ To a restaurant.

9. _____ A lot of cars.

10. _____ Her relatives and friends.

■ F. SPECIAL OCCASIONS
What is the special occasion in each photo? Describe what is happening. What are the people wearing?

Write about an important day in your life. What was the occasion? Who was there? Did you wear anything special? Why was this day important for you?

A. A TIME LINE *Think of seven important dates and events in your life, such as:*

I was born.

I came to the United States.

I got my driver's license.

Write the dates in the boxes below. Remember to put the dates in chronological order! Then write one sentence next to each date. Tell your partner about your life.

B. FIND SOMEONE WHO *Walk around the classroom and ask questions about growing up.*

EXAMPLE

Did you go to high school in the United States? No, I didn't. *(Keep asking!)*

Did you go to high school in the United States? Yes, I did. *(Write that student's name!)*

Find someone who . . . .   **Name**

1. went to high school in the United States.

2. had a pet.

3. spent time with his or her grandparents.

4. wore a uniform to school.

5. won a competition.

6. had a best friend.

7. went to a lot of parties.

8. failed his/her first driving test.

C. STUDENT TO STUDENT: The Wedding

Student A: *Turn to page 186. Read your partner questions 1 to 5.*

Student B: *Listen and write the questions on the line above the correct answer.*

<table>
<tr><td>Spelling Tips</td></tr>
</table>

Spelling Tips

wedding
get married
bridesmaids
reception

1. _____

   On July 8th.

2. _____

   At the First Baptist Church.

3. What time was the wedding? _____

   3:00.

4. _____

   Five.

5. _____

   Light pink.

Stop after number 5. **Student B** *will turn to page 186 and read questions 6 to 10.* **Student A** *will look below and write the questions above the correct answers.*

6. _____

   At the Sand's Restaurant.

7. _____

   At 5:00.

8. _____

   A hundred and fifty.

9. _____

   Chicken and shrimp.

10. _____

   Six thousand dollars.

■ A. WRITING QUESTIONS AND ANSWERS *Put these words in order. Write and then answer these questions about your life.*

1. _When were you born_ ? _____
   you / When / born / were ?

2. _____ ? _____
   Where / born / were / you ?

3. _____ ? _____
   live / Did / in / country / you / the ?

4. _____ ? _____
   start / When / you / did / school ?

5. _____ ? _____
   sport / play / Did / you / a / in high school ?

6. _____ ? _____
   drive / Who / how to / taught / you ?

7. _____ ? _____
   graduate / you / Did / high school / from ?

8. _____ ? _____
   When / to the United States / move / you / did ?

9. _____ ? _____
   alone / to the United States / come / you / Did ?

10. _____ ? _____
    you / move / to this state / did / Why ?

11. _____ ? _____
    your / was / Where / first job?

12. _____ ? _____
    When / this class / start / did / you ?

■ B. MICHAEL JORDAN *Ask and answer questions about Michael Jordan's life.*

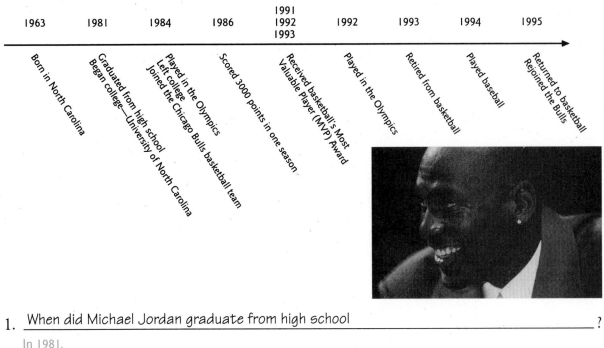

| 1963 | 1981 | 1984 | 1986 | 1991 1992 1993 | 1992 | 1993 | 1994 | 1995 |

Born in North Carolina
Graduated from high school
Began college—University of North Carolina
Played in the Olympics
Left college
Joined the Chicago Bulls basketball team
Scored 3000 points in one season
Received basketball's Most Valuable Player (MVP) Award
Played in the Olympics
Retired from basketball
Played baseball
Returned to basketball
Rejoined the Bulls

1. When did Michael Jordan graduate from high school _____?
   In 1981.

2. _____?
   The University of North Carolina.

3. _____?
   In 1984.

4. _____?
   The Chicago Bulls.

5. _____?
   Over 3000.

6. _____?
   In 1984 and again in 1992.

7. _____?
   Three times.

8. _____?
   In 1993.

9. _____?
   Because he wanted to play baseball.

10. _____?
    He returned to the Bulls.

What is Michael Jordan doing at this time? Is he still playing basketball? Name two other well-known basketball players.

A. MY TEACHER: A TIMELINE *Sit in small groups and prepare questions to ask your teacher about his or her life. Then, as a class, ask the questions and take notes. Make sure to write the years of important events. Draw a time line of the important events in your teacher's life and write a short paragraph about your teacher.*

B. MEMORIES *Bring in a photograph of an important day in your life, such as your graduation day, wedding day, a picture of you with your leg in a cast, etc. Tell your group or your classmates about this day. What happened that day? Your classmates should ask you questions, such as:*

How did you break your leg?

Did you stay in the hospital?

How long did you have a cast on your leg?

Did you stay home from school?

Who helped you?

C. THE BEST *Talk about some of the best times in your life. Sit in a group and complete one or more of these sentences. Give your group some more information about that person or experience.*

My best friend was _____ .

The best age to be was _____ .

The best teacher I ever had was _____ .

The best present I ever received was _____ .

The best place I ever lived was _____ .

The best day in my life was _____ .

The best vacation I ever took was to _____ .

1. *Yes/no* questions

Did you come to the United States last year?

Did	I you we they he she	come alone?

Yes, you did.   No, you didn't.
Yes, I did.   No, I didn't.
Yes, you did.   No, you didn't.
Yes, they did.   No, they didn't.
Yes, he did.   No, he didn't.
Yes, she did.   No, she didn't.

2. *Wh* questions

When did he come to Canada?

When Why How	did	I you we they he she	come to Canada?

3. *Who* questions (*who* as subject)

Who came last year?

Who	came	alone? with family? last year?

Around the House

Future Tense: *be going to*

A. HOUSEHOLD CHORES
Repeat these words and phrases after your teacher. Ask about any new words. Put the number of the correct picture next to each chore.

wash the dishes _____ pick up the books _____ wipe off the table _____

vacuum the living room _____ cook dinner _____ empty the basket _____

hang up the coats _____ dust _____ set the table _____

1	2	3
4	5	6
7	8	9

B. LISTEN: HOUSEHOLD CHORES

Mr. Grecco's parents are coming for a visit this evening and the house is a mess! Everyone has to work together to clean the kitchen and living room. Listen to the conversation between Mr. Grecco and the children. What is each person going to do?

Mr. Grecco

Mrs. Grecco

Aldo

Elena

C. WHO QUESTIONS

Ask and answer these questions about the conversation.

> EXAMPLE
>
> Who is going to cook dinner?   Mrs. Grecco is.

1. Who is going to vacuum the living room?
2. Who is going to dust the furniture?
3. Who is going to set the table?
4. Who is going to take out the garbage?

5. Who is going to hang up the coats?
6. Who is going to help in the kitchen?
7. Who is going to come for dinner?

D. LISTEN: FUTURE VERBS

*Listen and write the future verb you hear. You are going to hear each sentence twice, once with **going to** and once with the reduced form **gonna**. Write the verb with **be going to**.*

> EXAMPLE
>
> Mrs. Grecco **is going to** cook dinner.

1. The children _____ are going to clean _____ downstairs.

2. Aldo _____ the books.

3. He _____ the carpet, too.

4. Elena _____ the furniture.

5. She _____ the table, too.

6. Mr. and Mrs. Grecco _____ in the kitchen.

7. Mr. Grecco _____ the dirty dishes.

8. He _____ a salad, too.

◼ E. CONTRAST: FUTURE AND PRESENT CONTINUOUS *Read each sentence.*
If it describes right now, circle **Now.** *If it describes the future, circle* **Future.**

1. The children are watching TV.	(Now)	Future
2. Their father is talking to them.	Now	Future
3. Elena is going to clean the living room.	Now	Future
4. Aldo is going to empty the baskets.	Now	Future
5. Mrs. Grecco is cooking a big dinner.	Now	Future
6. Mr. Grecco's parents are going to come for dinner.	Now	Future
7. They're driving to their son's house.	Now	Future
8. They're going to arrive soon.	Now	Future

Working Together

◼ A. THE ROOMMATES *Sit in a group of three students. Imagine that you are roommates and your apartment is a mess. Divide the chores. Write a name under each chore.*

■ B. ANSWER *Answer these questions about the chores on page 160. Use **it** or **them** in your answer.*

1. Who's going to empty the baskets?
2. Who's going to wash the dishes?
3. Who's going to mop the floor?
4. Who's going to clean the bathroom?
5. Who's going to wash the towels?
6. Who's going to vacuum the carpets?
7. Who's going to do the food shopping?

■ C. FUTURE SITUATIONS *Talk about each situation. What's going to happen?*

■■

D. STUDENT TO STUDENT *You each have part of Mrs. Grecco's schedule for next week. Ask and answer questions about her calendar. Complete the schedule.*

Student A: *Use the calendar below.*

Student B: *Use the calendar on page 187.*

Student B: *Use the calendar on page 187.*

EXAMPLE

A: What's she going to do on Monday afternoon?

B: She's going to take Elena to the dentist.

	Monday	Tuesday	Wednesday	Thursday	Friday
morning	Work Art Gallery	Work Art Gallery	Work Art Gallery	Work Art Gallery	Work Art Gallery
afternoon	Elena— dentist		Watch Aldo's soccer game		
evening	Go to an art show		Do her art assignment		Go to her sister's birthday party

Practicing on Your Own

A. FUTURE TIME EXPRESSIONS *Answer these questions with a future time expression. Use **it, them, him** or **her** in your answer.*

in a little while	tomorrow	soon
in a few minutes	the day after tomorrow	later
in an hour	next week	this evening
in a few weeks	next month	tonight

1. When are you going to clean your room?

   I'm going to clean it in a few minutes.

2. When are you going to see the dentist?

   _____

3. When are you going to pay the bills?

   _____

4. When are you going to wash the car?

_____

5. When are you going to paint the bathroom?

_____

6. When are you going to call your sister?

_____

7. When are you going to register your car?

_____

8. When are you going to speak with the boss?

_____

9. When are you going to deposit your paycheck?

_____

10. When are you going to fix the car?

_____

■ B. PARENT AND TEENAGER *Complete these conversations between a parent and a teenager.*

1. The Messy Bedroom

   Parent: Your room is a mess! When are you going to clean it?

   Teenager: _I'm going to clean it tonight._____

   Parent: When are you going to wash your clothes?

   Teenager: _____

2. Homework

   Parent: When are you going to do your homework?

   Teenager: _____

   Parent: When are you going to get your report card?

   Teenager: _____

3. What's for Dinner?

   Teenager: I'm starving! When are we going to eat?

   Parent: _____

   Teenager: What are we going to have?

   Parent: _____

4. Going Out

Teenager: Can I go out with my friends tonight?

Parent: Where are you going to go?

Teenager: _____

Parent: Who are you going to go with?

Teenager: _____

Parent: How are you going to get there?

Teenager: _____

Parent: What time are you going to be home?

Teenager: _____

Parent: _____

Having Fun with the Language

A. GUESSING GAME *What do you think your partner is going to do this weekend? Make guesses. Then, read your guesses to your partner. Check if each guess was right or wrong.*

EXAMPLE

Student A: I think you are going to visit your friends.

Student B: You're wrong. I'm not going to visit anyone.

				Right	Wrong
1. I	think	don't think	you are going to visit your friends.	❏	❏
2. I	think	don't think	you are going to go to a party.	❏	❏
3. I	think	don't think	you are going to wash your car.	❏	❏
4. I	think	don't think	you are going to leave the state.	❏	❏
5. I	think	don't think	you are going to call your mother.	❏	❏
6. I	think	don't think	you are going to rent a video.	❏	❏
7. I	think	don't think	you are going to take some photographs.	❏	❏
8. I	think	don't think	you are going to clean your apartment.	❏	❏
9. I	think	don't think	you are going to order a pizza.	❏	❏
10. I	think	don't think	you are going to _____.	❏	❏

B. CATEGORIES

Read each list of items. What is this person going to do or to make? Then, sit in a group and write three more groups of words. Read your list to another group or to the class. Can they guess what you are going to do?

ticket	paper	hammer
passport	pen	saw
suitcase	stamp	nails
	envelope	wood

Grammar Summary

1. Future tense
Use *be + going to* to talk about actions in the future.

2. Some future time expressions
Put the time expression at the beginning or the end of a sentence.

Next week I'm going to visit my brother.

I'm going to visit my brother **next week.**

tonight	next week	in a few minutes
tomorrow	next month	in a little while
the day after tomorrow	next year	in a few hours
		in a week
		in a month

3. Statements

I	am		
We You They	are	going to	work. clean.
He She It	is		help.

Negatives

I	am not		
We You They	are not aren't	going to	work. clean.
He She It	is not isn't		help.

4. Pronunciation note

Going to is often pronounced **gonna.**

When writing, use **going to.** Do not write **gonna.**

18 Vacation

Future Tense Questions: *be going to*

A. LISTEN: VACATION PLANS *Listen to the vacation plans of each student and complete the information in the boxes.*

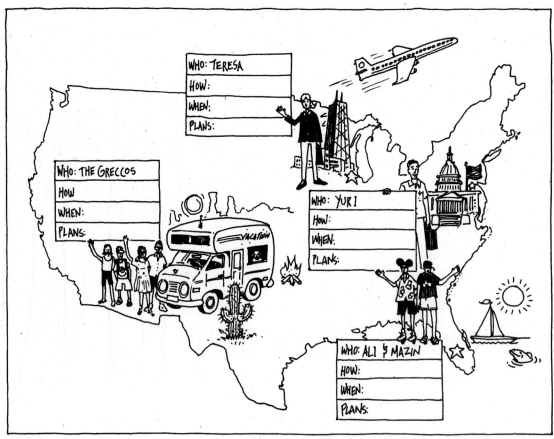

■■

B. LISTEN: QUESTIONS *Listen to the questions about Teresa's and the Greccos' vacation plans. Circle the answer.*

1. (a.) To Chicago.   b. By train.   c. On July 1st.
2. a. Teresa is.   b. Her sister.   c. The Art Institute.
3. a. On July 1st.   b. By train.   c. For ten days.
4. a. Visit her sister.   b. On July 1st.   c. Once a year.
5. a. On July 1st.   b. By train.   c. On July 10th.
6. a. Once a year.   b. For ten days.   c. With her sister.
7. a. To the Southwest.   b. For a month.   c. In a camper.
8. a. To the national parks. b. On July 15th.   c. By camper.
9. a. Visit the national parks. b. Stay in the camper. c. Reservations.
10. a. On July 15th.   b. For a month.   c. Every summer.

■ C. ANSWER *Answer these questions about the students' vacation plans.*

| EXAMPLE |

Is he going to fly?   **Is she going to drive?**   **Are they going to rent a car?**

Yes, he is.   Yes, she is.   Yes, they are.

No, he isn't.   No, she isn't.   No, they aren't.

1. Is Yuri going to fly to Washington, D.C.?
2. Is he going to travel alone?
3. Is he going to stay for a week?
4. Is Ali going to stay in Orlando for a week?
5. Is he going to fly?
6. Is his friend going to travel with him?
7. Are the Greccos going to drive to San Francisco?
8. Are they going to stay in motels every night?
9. Is Teresa going to visit her sister?
10. Is she going to stay in Chicago for two weeks?

■ D. ASK AND ANSWER *Ask and answer questions about these students' vacation plans.*

Where				go?
How	is	Yuri		get there?
What			going to	do?
How long	are	Ali and Mazin		stay?
When				return?

167

Working Together

■ A. MATCH *Match each picture with the name of the correct city.*

Chicago   Boston   New York City   San Francisco

■ B. CHECK *What do you like to do when you visit a new city? Check the activities you enjoy, and then read your sentences to a partner.*

- ❑ I like to visit art museums.
- ❑ I like to go sightseeing.
- ❑ I like to visit the zoo.
- ❑ I like to go shopping.
- ❑ I like to see historical places.

- ❑ I like to visit science museums.
- ❑ I like to eat out.
- ❑ I like to walk in the parks.
- ❑ I like to see shows or movies.
- ❑ I like to go to concerts.

■ C. PLAN A VACATION *Choose a city you would like to visit on your next vacation. Sit in a group of three or four students who would like to go to the same city. Plan a vacation. You need to decide this information.*

1. What city are you going to visit?
2. How are you going to get there?
3. How long are you going to stay?
4. When are you going to leave and return?
5. Where are you going to stay?
6. How much money are you going to take?
7. What are you going to do?
8. What are you going to buy?

Tell another group your vacation plans.

■ D. THE TOP TEN *In her book,* Vacation Places Rated, *Sylvia McNair gives her recommendations for the top ten vacation areas in the United States. These areas offer parks, beautiful scenery, museums, historical sites, sports, or a variety of other activities.*

Talk about the vacation areas. Use these sentences to help you.

1. The most popular vacation area in the United States

   is _____ .

2. _____ is more popular than _____ .

3. There are a lot of things to do in _____ .

4. In _____ , you can _____ .

5. I think _____ is popular because _____ .

6. I was never in _____ .

7. On my next vacation, I'm going to _____

   because _____ .

Top Ten Areas
1. Seattle
2. Los Angeles
3. Hawaii
4. Miami
5. San Francisco
6. Boston
7. Chicago
8. Denver
9. New York City
10. Tampa Bay

■ A. WRITE THE QUESTION *Write questions about these vacation plans.*

Who: Teresa

How: Train

Where: Chicago

When: July 1–10

Plans: Art Institute, Science Museum, baseball game

Who: Ali and Mazin

How: Plane

Where: Florida

When: August 10–17

Plans: Disneyworld, Epcot Center, Universal Studios, Sea World

1. _____Who is going to visit Chicago_____? Teresa is.

2. _____? To Chicago.

3. _____? On July 1.

4. _____? For ten days.

5. _____? See a baseball game.

6. _____? Ali and Mazin are.

7. _____? Florida.

8. _____? By plane.

9. _____? On August 17.

10. _____? Disneyland.

■ B. COMPLETE THE STORY *Fill in the verbs in the correct tense.*

Mr. and Mrs. Grecco _____are_____ (be) both teachers and they _____ (negative–work) in July and August. So, every summer, they _____ (take) a long vacation. Next summer, they _____ (go) west and _____ (stay) in two of the country's most beautiful national parks.

The Greccos _____ (live) in Boston, and they _____ (drive) two thousand miles. Mr. and Mrs. Grecco _____ (share) the driving. On the way, they _____ (stop) and _____ (visit) relatives in Chicago. Some of the

drive _____ (be) very interesting, but some of it _____ (be) boring.

Elena _____ (bring) her Walkman® and many tapes. Aldo _____

(take) his Nintendo® games.

The Greccos already _____ (have) reservations in both Yellowstone National

Park and the Grand Canyon. They _____ (stay) in each park for a week. They

_____ (hike) and _____ (swim) at both parks. At Yellowstone, they

_____ (rent) bicycles for two days. At the Grand Canyon, they _____

(take) a three-day raft ride down the Colorado River. Mrs. Grecco _____ (bring)

her camera. She _____ (take) pictures of the wildlife in the national parks. Mr.

Grecco and Elena _____ (fish), and then they _____ (have) fresh fish

for dinner.

No pets are allowed in the parks, so the Greccos _____ (negative–bring) their

dog. He's _____ (stay) back in Boston with Aldo's grandparents. Aldo

_____ (be) unhappy about this.

■ C. WRITE THE QUESTION *Write questions about the Greccos' vacation plans.*

1. _____How far are they going to drive_____? Two thousand miles.

2. _____? In Chicago.

3. _____? Their relatives.

4. _____? Her Walkman®.

5. _____? For a week.

6. _____? Bicycles.

7. _____? A three day raft trip.

8. _____? Pictures of wildlife.

9. _____? No, they aren't.

10. _____? Aldo's grandparents.

A. TRAVEL POSTER *Make a travel poster of your country or the area you live in now. Use the following as a guide. You can add a simple map of your country, pictures, post cards, or other information to make your poster interesting.*

Enjoy Beautiful _____

on Your Next Vacation!

Spend time at _____ . (park)

Tour _____ . (historic place)

Lie in the sun on our beautiful beaches in _____ . (city or town)

Have a wonderful time in _____ . (fun place)

Take a ride along the _____ . (river)

See the exhibits at _____ . (museum)

Climb _____ . (mountain)

Enjoy the _____ . (festival)

Relax at _____ . (hotel)

Try delicious _____ food, such as

_____ or _____ .

At night, dance to _____ music at

_____ . (club)

◼ B. WHAT IS IT? WHERE IS IT? *Can you identify each of these popular vacation places?*
What is each one? Where is it?

amusement park	area	national park
historical site	skyscraper	monument

Epcot Center	Haleakala	The Alamo
Disneyland	The World Trade Center	Yellowstone
Graceland	Disney World	Sears Tower
The Grand Canyon	Niagara Falls	The Statue of Liberty
Williamsburg	The White House	The Everglades
Hollywood	The Liberty Bell	Chinatown

Grammar Summary

1. *Yes/no questions*

Am I **going to see** you?	....	Yes, you are.	No, you aren't.
Are you **going to stay?**	....	Yes, I am.	No, I'm not.
Is he **going to go** alone?	....	Yes, he is.	No, he isn't.
Is it **going to be** hot?	....	Yes, it is.	No, it isn't.
Are we **going to leave?**	....	Yes, you are.	No, you aren't.
Are you **going to go?**	....	Yes, we are.	No, we aren't.
Are they **going to drive?**	....	Yes, they are.	No, they aren't.

2. *Wh questions*

When **am I going to leave?**	...	Tomorrow from 4:00 to 9:00.
What **are** you **going to do?**	...	Visit the White House.
How long **is she going to stay?**	...	For a week.
When **is** it **going to leave?**	...	At 6:00.
Where **are** we **going to go?**	...	To Chicago.
How **are** you **going to get** there?	...	By bus.
Where **are** they **going to stay?**	...	In a motel.

# Appendix

Days of the week

Sunday
Monday
Tuesday
Wednesday
Thursday
Friday
Saturday

Months of the year

January	July
February	August
March	September
April	October
May	November
June	December

Numbers 1–100

one	eleven	ten
two	twelve	twenty
three	thirteen	thirty
four	fourteen	forty
five	fifteen	fifty
six	sixteen	sixty
seven	seventeen	seventy
eight	eighteen	eighty
nine	nineteen	ninety
ten	twenty	one hundred

Other numbers

21	twenty-one	66	sixty-six
27	twenty-seven	75	seventy-five
35	thirty-five	84	eighty-four
46	forty-six	99	ninety-nine
53	fifty-three	100	one hundred

Irregular past verbs

be	was/were	let	let
become	became	lose	lost
begin	began	make	made
break	broke	pay	paid
bring	brought	put	put
buy	bought	read	read
choose	chose	ride	rode
come	came	run	ran
cost	cost	say	said
cut	cut	see	saw
do	did	sell	sold
draw	drew	send	sent
drink	drank	set	set
drive	drove	sing	sang
eat	ate	sit	sat
fall	fell	sleep	slept
feel	felt	speak	spoke
find	found	spend	spent
fly	flew	stand	stood
forget	forgot	swim	swam
get	got	take	took
give	gave	teach	taught
go	went	tell	told
hang	hung	think	thought
have	had	understand	understood
hold	held	wear	wore
know	knew	win	won
leave	left	write	wrote

Prepositions of Place

in

room	– in the living room
	– in the kitchen
	– in Room 511
	– on Park Avenue
city	– in Boston
state	– in New Jersey
country	– in the United States
	– in Mexico

in the yard

in the basement

in the attic

in the garage

in the car

in the corner	– in the corner of the room
	– in the corner of your paper

in the front

in the back

at

building	– at the bank
	– at the post office
	– at the supermarket

at home

at work

at church

at school

at a **specific** address –

   at **227** Broad Street

   at **37** Park Avenue

at the bus stop

on

street	– on Broad Street
	– on Park Avenue
floor	– on the second floor

on the porch

on the corner	– on the corner of Park Avenue and Main Street

on the bus

on the train

on the plane

on the left

on the right

on the top

on the bottom

on the side

Do not use prepositions with...

downtown

uptown

downstairs

upstairs

inside

outside

Note:

For a street: The bank is **on** Broad Street.

For a specific address: The bank is **at** 227 Broad Street.

Prepositions of Time

in

month	– in February
	– in September
season	– in the winter
	– in the fall
year	– in 1965
	– in 1994

in the morning
in the afternoon
in the evening
in two days
in a week
in an hour
in a little while
in a hurry

at

exact time	– at 9:15
	– at nine-fifteen
	– at 12:30
	– at twelve-thirty

at noon
at night
at midnight
at the moment

Note:

For a month:	**in** May
For a year:	**in** 1998
For a date:	**on** May 7 *or* **on** May 7, 1995
For a day:	**on** Sunday

on

day	– on Monday
	– on Sunday
specific day	– on Thanksgiving
date	– on February 7
	– on November 10, 1973

on the weekend
on time

from   to

–from 8:00 to 12:00
–from Monday to Friday
–from 1990 to 1998

Do not use prepositions with...

last night
last May
tomorrow
yesterday
this weekend
next week
tonight

Cut-out Appendix

Chapter 4, page 35

Chapter 6, page 51

Student to Student Exercises

Unit 1, page 6

Student B: *Read sentences 1 to 10 to Student A.*

Student B	Student A
1. He is a student.	11. She is married.
2. She isn't at school	12. He isn't at work.
3. We aren't from Russia.	13. We are at school.
4. I'm not married.	14. Boston is a city.
5. You are in Room 2.	15. It isn't in Mexico.
6. They aren't at work.	16. She isn't from China.
7. She is single.	17. I'm not a teacher.
8. I'm a student.	18. He is 20 years old.
9. It isn't Monday.	19. We are at school.
10. They are from Japan.	20. You are in class.

When you finish, Student A will read sentences 11 to 20 above. Student B will circle the correct verb on page 6.

Unit 4, page 36

Student B: *Look at the list of answers below. Student A will ask you questions. The answers are not in order. Give your partner the correct answer from the first list.*

Student B	Student A
She's 27.	It's brown.
Mary.	They're brown.
They're blue.	Kathy.
It's red.	July 5th.
Wilson.	She's a waitress.
Chicago.	She's 35.
She's an accountant.	Casini.
March 10th.	San Diego.

When you finish, Student B will ask the questions on page 36 and Student A will give the answers from the second list above.

Unit 5, page 42

Student B: *Read the sentences below to Student A.*

Student B:

1. There are two plates on the table.
2. The pot is on the stove.
3. The toaster is on the counter next to the refrigerator.
4. There are two glasses in the sink.
5. There are two cups on the table.
6. The clock is over the stove.
7. The refrigerator is between the stove and the table.

When you finish, turn to page 42. Student A will read the sentences below.

Student A:

1. The pot is on the counter next to the sink.
2. There are two glasses on the table.
3. The blender is on the counter.
4. The cat is on the refrigerator.
5. There are three chairs in the kitchen.
6. There are two plants on the counter.
7. The bowl of fruit is on the table.

Student B: *Look at the map below. Ask Student A about the location of these places. Do not look at Student A's map.*

the laundromat   the hospital

the car wash   the jewelry store

the movie theater   the Italian restaurant

EXAMPLE

A: Where's the Mexican restaurant?

B: It's on the corner of Second Street and River Road, next to the barber.

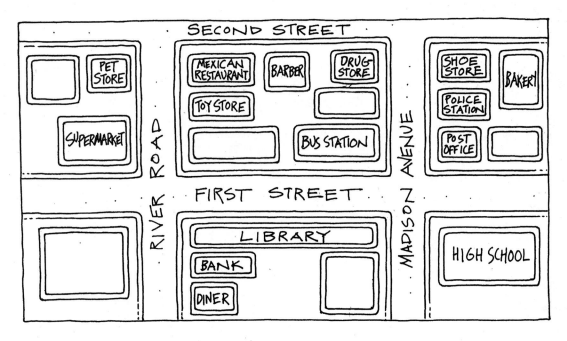

Unit 7, page 58

Student A: *Read the seven sentences below to your partner.*

Student A	Student B
1. We have class in the morning.	1. Our teacher is a man.
2. Our class begins at 9:00.	2. The teacher comes late.
3. Three students speak Japanese.	3. The teacher gives a lot of homework.
4. We have a break.	4. The teacher drinks coffee in class.
5. We have class three days a week.	5. The teacher speaks Spanish.
6. This class is two hours long.	6. The teacher has long hair.
7. Our classroom is on the first floor.	7. The teacher wears glasses.

When you finish, turn to page 58. Student B will read seven new sentences in the second column.

Student A and Student B both have pictures of the same classroom. Do not look at one another's picture! There are seven differences in your pictures. Talk about your pictures and try to find the differences.

Student B: *Look at the picture below.*
Student A: *Turn to page 87. Look at the classroom picture.*

Menu Prices

Ask about the price of each item and complete your menu.
Student A: *Look at the menu below.*
Student B: *Look at the menu on page 97.*

$1.29 = a dollar twenty-nine
one dollar and twenty-nine cents
$3.50 = three fifty
three dollars and fifty cents

EXAMPLE

A: How much is a hamburger?

B: A dollar forty-nine.

MENU

Hamburger	$1.49	French fries	small	
Cheeseburger			large	
Super Burger		Drink	small	.89
Chicken Sandwich	3.59		medium	1.09
Fish Sandwich	2.99		large	
Chicken Pieces		Coffee		.79
Salad bar	3.49	Apple pie		

Student A: *Read the eight sentences below to your partner.*

Student A	Student B
a. There's one pencil on this desk.	a. There are two pencils on this desk.
b. There are two erasers on this desk.	b. There aren't any pencils on this desk.
c. There are two dictionaries on this desk.	c. There aren't any dictionaries on this desk.
d. There's a can of soda on this desk.	d. There isn't any coffee on this desk.
e. There are five pencils on this desk.	e. There are some keys on this desk.
f. There isn't any paper on this desk.	f. There's a lot of paper on this desk.
g. There is a pair of glasses on this desk.	g. There is a piece of paper on this desk.
h. There are some books on this desk.	h. There is a pack of gum on this desk.

When you finish, turn to page 108. Student B will read the eight sentences in the second column.

Unit 15, page 140

Student A: *Read these sentences to Student B. Tell your partner: These sentences are about this morning.*

1. You got up late.
2. You took a shower this morning.
3. You drank a glass of orange juice for breakfast.
4. You ate a donut.
5. You walked to school today.
6. You found a dollar on the sidewalk.
7. You forgot your English book.

When you finish, turn to page 140.

Student B: *Tell your partner: These sentences are about last night.*

1. You had chicken for dinner last night.
2. You did your homework.
3. You watched TV last night.
4. You took a bath.
5. You called a friend.
6. You listened to the radio.
7. You went to bed at midnight.

Unit 16, page 153
The Wedding

Student A: *Read your partner questions 1 to 5.*

1. What time was the wedding?
2. How many bridesmaids did she have?
3. When did Monica and Stan get married?
4. What color did the bridesmaids wear?
5. Where did they get married?

Stop after number 5. Student A will turn to page 153. Student B will read questions 6 to 10.

Student B

6. What time was the reception?
7. How much did the reception cost?
8. What did they serve at the reception?
9. Where was the reception?
10. How many people came to the reception?

You each have part of Mrs. Grecco's schedule for next week. Ask and answer questions about her calendar.
Complete the schedule.

Student A: Use the calendar on page 162. **Student B:** Use the calendar below.

> **EXAMPLE**
>
> Student A: What's she going to do on Monday afternoon?
>
> Student B: She's going to take Elena to the dentist.

	Monday	Tuesday	Wednesday	Thursday	Friday
morning	Work Art Gallery	Work Art Gallery	Work Art Gallery	Work Art Gallery	Work Art Gallery
afternoon	Take Elena to the dentist	Visit parents		Buy a present for her sister	Bake a cake for her sister's birthday
evening		Take art classes		Work Art Gallery	

Tape Script

Unit 1, page 2

B. Listen: Personal Information Listen to the information about each picture. Write **Yes** or **No** on the line before each statement.

PICTURE 1

My name is Ana Luisa. I'm from Guadalajara, Mexico. I'm eighteen years old and I'm single. I'm a college student and I'm walking to class.

PICTURE 2

This is Kashif. He's from Pakistan. He's twenty-five and he's single. He's a student, but he isn't at school now. He's at work.

PICTURE 3

This is Kim and this is Su-Jin. They're from Seoul, the capital of Korea. Kim is thirty-four and Su-Jin is twenty-nine. They're married. They have one child, a little girl. Kim and Su-Jin aren't at school now. They're at home.

PICTURE 4

I am from Mexico, but now I live in Texas. Texas is in the south. It's a big state. I live in San Antonio. San Antonio isn't the capital of Texas. Austin is the capital.

Unit 2, page 14

B. Listen: People and Places Listen to the tape and write four adjectives under each picture.

PICTURE 1

This is Anna. She's a student in my class. She's from Russia. Anna's tall and thin. She's at school now. Anna's a good student. She's hardworking and serious. And she's always busy.

PICTURE 2

This is Edgar and Maria Aquino. They're in my class, too. They're from the Philippines and they're married. Edgar and Maria are at a restaurant with their little girl. It's a hot day and they're hot and tired. They're very thirsty and they're very hungry, too.

PICTURE 3

This is my country, Mexico. Mexico is south of the United States and it's very large. Mexico is hot all the time. The capital is Mexico City. Mexico City is very large. The population is about seven million. Mexico City is always noisy and busy. I think Mexican people are friendly.

Unit 3 page 22

A. Listen: The Classroom Listen to this classroom vocabulary. Write *a* or *an* for each word.

1. a book	7. a dictionary	13. a desk
2. a student	8. a ruler	14. an apple
3. a pencil	9. an eraser	15. a backpack
4. an umbrella	10. a pencil sharpener	16. a chair
5. a notebook	11. a man	17. a computer
6. a pen	12. a woman	18. a map
		19. a clock
		20. a calculator

page 24

D. Listen: Singular or Plural Listen and circle the word you hear.

1. books	6. a door
2. a pencil	7. tables
3. a student	8. dictionaries
4. windows	9. a man
5. clocks	10. women

Unit 4, page 31

B. Listen: Family Relationships Listen to the tape and fill in the family relationships.

1. Pedro is Rosa's husband.	5. Olga is Tom's mother.
2. David is Pedro and Rosa's son.	6. Kathy is Tom's sister.
3. David is Stella's brother.	7. Stella is Tom and Kathy's aunt.
4. Stella is Rosa's daughter.	8. Tom is Stella's nephew.

page 32

D. Listen: Possessive Adjectives Listen to the tape and complete these sentences with **she** or **her**.

1. This is my little sister.
2. Her name is Maria.
3. She's sixteen years old today, but her birthday is next week.
4. Her eyes are brown and her hair is long and brown.
5. She's in tenth grade.

Listen to the tape and complete these sentences with **he** or **his**.

1. This is my brother.
2. His name is David.
3. He's nineteen years old and he's in college.
4. His birthday is on October 2nd.
5. He's on the baseball team.

Listen to the tape and complete these sentences with **they** or **their**.

1. This is my brother Steve and his wife, Sue.
2. They're married and they live in Florida.
3. Their home is in Miami.
4. They have two children. Their names are Brian and Kevin.

Unit 5, page 41

B. Listen: Prepositions *Listen and write the preposition you hear.*

1. The sofa is in the living room.
2. The end table is next to the sofa.
3. The books are on the coffee table.
4. The lamp is on the end table.
5. The picture is over the sofa.
6. The dresser is in the bedroom.
7. The night table is between the bed and the dresser.
8. The shoes are under the bed.
9. The table is in the kitchen.
10. The basket is next to the sink.
11. The window is over the sink.
12. The cabinets are next to the refrigerator.
13. The cat is on the chair.
14. The remote control is on the table.

Unit 6, page 49

B. Listen: Stores *Listen and write the name of the store in each sentence.*

1. Jae Hoon is at the bookstore.
2. Esperanza is at the supermarket.
3. Marek and Beata are at the diner.
4. Brian is at the barber shop.
5. Lisa is on Main Street, at the bank.
6. Mr. and Mrs. Garcia are at the department store.
7. Sara is at drugstore.

page 49

C. Listen: Locations *Listen to the location of each place and write it on the map below.*

1. There's a laundromat between the shoe store and the jewelry store.
2. A small park is next to the hospital.
3. There's a bank across from the park.
4. The bus station is on the corner of Center Street and Mountain Avenue.
5. There's a diner between the post office and the bank.
6. There's a drug store next to the shoe store.
7. The police station is next to the bus station.
8. The library is on Mountain Avenue, next to the post office.

Unit 7, page 54

A. Listen: A Daily Schedule *Listen to the story about a typical day for Susan and Paul. Write the time on each clock.*

Susan and Paul are a young married couple. They have a busy week. They both get up at 7:00 in the morning. At 7:30 they eat a small breakfast, usually toast and juice. Susan drinks tea; Paul drinks coffee. At 8:00 they leave for work. Susan walks because she lives near her office and she likes the exercise. Paul drives because he lives 15 miles from work. They both work from 9:00 to 5:00, and they get home at about 6:00. On Monday and Wednesday, they go to school at a community college in their area. Their classes begin at 7:00. Susan studies nursing, and Paul studies computer science. They arrive home at 10:00. It's a long day, so they're usually tired. They talk and relax. Sometimes they study or Susan reads and Paul watches TV until 11:30. At midnight, they go to bed.

B. Listen: Present Tense *Listen and write the present tense verb you hear.*

1. Susan and Paul get up at 7:00.
2. They eat breakfast at 7:30.
3. Susan walks to work.
4. Paul drives to work.
5. Paul works 15 miles from home.
6. They go to school.
7. Susan studies nursing.
8. After class, Susan reads.
9. Paul watches TV.
10. They go to sleep at 12:00.

Unit 8, page 64

B. Listen: Job Information *Listen to Mateo and Ela talk about their jobs. Complete the information.*

I am a waiter at La Casita, a Mexican restaurant. It's a large restaurant with forty tables. La Casita is open for both lunch and dinner. I work six days a week from 4:00 to 1:00 a.m. and I often work later on Friday and Saturday nights. The restaurant is busy all the time. I usually work six tables. First, I tell the customers the specials and then I take their orders. I only make three dollars an hour, but I make a lot of money in tips. I am friendly and the customers like me. Many of my customers are American, so I speak a lot of English at work. On the weeknights, I make forty or fifty dollars in tips. On the weekends, I make over a hundred dollars in tips.

I am a travel agent. I work part time at a travel agency in town. I work from Thursday to Sunday, from 12:00 to 6:00. I help people make vacation plans. I sell airline tickets, make hotel and car reservations, and give people information about travel. Most of my customers are Polish, so I speak Polish most of the time. But when I call the airlines or different hotels, I have to speak English. I sit at my desk and use a computer for a lot of my work. I get three weeks vacation. And when I travel, I get a 50% discount on my airline tickets and hotel reservations.

Unit 9, page 75

C. Listen: Count and Non-count Nouns *Listen and write the name of each food in the correct column.*

1. some apples	6. an orange	11. some bread
2. an apple	7. some oranges	12. some juice
3. some rice	8. some oil	13. some milk
4. some ice cream	9. an egg	14. a cookie
5. some bananas	10. some donuts	15. a cake

E. Listen: A Shopping List *Listen to this couple talk about the food that they need at the supermarket. Circle the items they need. Cross out the items they don't need.*

M: What do we need at the store?
W: Not too much. I went to the store a few days ago. We need fruit—apples, bananas, but we don't need any oranges. There are four in the refrigerator. And we have a pineapple, too.
M: How about milk and juice?
W: Milk, yes. We always need milk. But we have orange juice and apple juice.
M: What about meat?
W: Get some chicken and some pork chops. We don't need any beef.
M: Okay.
W: There's a sale on paper products. Get about four rolls of toilet paper and two boxes of tissues. But we don't need any paper towels.
M: Any cereal?
W: Let's see. There are three boxes in the cabinet. But we need rice and spaghetti.
M: Anything else?
W: Yes, some fresh vegetables, any kind you like. And pick up some ice cream for the kids.
M: I never forget the ice cream.

B: Listen: Classroom Activities *It's 8:55 and class begins at 9:00. These students are in the class a few minutes early. Listen and write the names on the correct person.*

This is English 1. It's 8:55 in the morning. Class begins in five minutes. Some of the students are already in class. Carlos and Rosa are always the first students in class. Right now, they're sitting and talking about the weather. It's really cold today. They're both from Mexico and they're speaking Spanish. Carlos is eating a banana and Rosa is drinking a cup of coffee. Maria is sitting alone. She's studying for a test today. Marc is sitting alone, too. He's doing his homework. Marc always does his homework in class. Linn is standing at the blackboard and writing the day and the date. She writes this information on the blackboard every morning. David and Vin are standing near the window and talking about baseball. They're speaking English, because Vin speaks Vietnamese and David speaks Spanish. Ali is reading the newspaper. He walks to school and buys the newspaper on the way. He always reads the news before class. Adam is walking into the classroom. He's wearing a hat and coat because it's cold out today. He's carrying his books. He's smiling and saying, "Hi!" to the other students.

C. Listen: Present Continuous Verbs *Listen and write the verb you hear.*

1. Carlos is talking to Rosa.
2. He is eating a donut.
3. Rosa is drinking a cup of coffee.
4. Carlos and Rosa are sitting in the classroom.
5. Maria is studying for a test.
6. Marc isn't reading a book. He is doing his homework.
7. Vin isn't speaking Vietnamese. He is speaking English.
8. The students aren't studying French. They're studying English.

B: Listen: Lunch Time *Listen and write the name on the correct person in the fast food restaurant.*

It's 12:30 and it's lunch time at Mr. Burger. Teresa is working at the counter. She's taking Patty's order. Patty is ordering a chicken sandwich and a soda. Teresa is calling the order back to the kitchen. Patty is paying for her order, she's handing Teresa a ten-dollar bill. It's early and the line is short. Kathy Green is standing in line in back of Patty. She's with her son, Tommy. She's holding his hand. Kathy is tired from shopping all morning. Tommy is tired and hungry. He's crying. Kim is sitting at a table with her two sons, Jason and Todd. Kim isn't hungry. She's only drinking a cup of coffee. Jason and Todd are always eating. They each have two hamburgers. The boys are telling their mother about their soccer game. Ken and Ray are in the kitchen. They're cooking hamburgers. It's hot today and Ken and Ray are very hot, standing over the grill.

D. Listen: questions *Listen and write the question you hear. Then, circle the correct answer.*

1. Who is ordering lunch?
2. What is Teresa doing?
3. What is Patty ordering?
4. Why is Tommy crying?
5. Where are Ken and Ray working?

C. **Listen to Prices** *Listen and write the prices you hear.*

EXAMPLE

$1.29 a dollar and twenty-nine cents *or* one dollar and twenty-nine cents

$3.50 three fifty *or* three dollars and fifty cents

1. ninety-nine cents
2. a dollar twenty-nine
3. a dollar sixty-nine
4. two fifty
5. two thirty-nine

6. two eighty-five
7. three forty-nine
8. four seventy-two
9. six ninety-five

A. **Listen:** **Ordering Lunch** *Listen to this conversation between a counter clerk and a customer. Fill in the missing words.*

1: Can I help you?

2: Sure. I'd like a chicken sandwich and a soda.

1: What size soda—small, medium, or large?

2: Medium.

1: Anything else?

2: Umm. A small fries.

1: That's it?

2: Yes.

1: For here or to go?

2: To go.

1: That's a chicken sandwich, medium soda, and small fries. That's $6.85.

Unit 12, page 105

B. **Listen:** **The School** *Listen to these sentences about the school and circle Yes or No.*

1. There are two mailboxes in front of the building.
2. There are a lot of cars in the parking lot.
3. There are a few students walking into the school.
4. There is one security guard in the security booth.
5. There are three students at the bus stop.
6. There are two students sitting on a bench.
7. There is a statue in front of this building.
8. There is a flag next to the statue.

C. Listen: Quantifiers *Listen and complete these sentences with* **is** *or* **are** *and an expression from the box on the right.*

1. There is a telephone booth next to the building.
2. There isn't a bus at the bus stop.
3. There is one security guard in the booth.
4. There are three floors in the building.
5. There are a few benches outside.
6. There are some students going into the building.
7. There are several garbage cans outside.
8. There are many students outside the building.
9. There are a lot of cars in the parking lot.
10. There aren't any students at the bus stop.

Unit 13, page 115

C. Listen: A Weather Report *Listen to the weather report. Put the correct picture and temperature for each city on the map.*

The national weather map shows unsettled weather in the north and hotter weather throughout most of the south. Let's look first at the Northeast. In Boston, it's warm and raining. The temperature is 50°. We expect this weather to continue for the next two days. New York is a warm 63°. But it's cloudy and the rain should begin there sometime tonight. Washington, D.C. is also warm and cloudy. The temperature there is 72°. Looking west, the weather picture remains overcast. It's very windy in Chicago today and the temperature is only 38°. Looking up at the northwest corner of the country, it is raining in Seattle with a temperature of 58°. We're sorry, Seattle. This rain will continue for the next few days. And it's a cold, wet day in Denver, with a temperature of only 42°. If you want to enjoy warm, sunny skies, you'll have to travel south. The weather map for the southern part of the country is picture perfect. In Los Angeles, it's sunny with a temperature of 80°. San Diego is enjoying the same sunny weather and the temperature there is a comfortable 84°. Houston is a little cloudy and the temperature there is 73°. But the clouds should be leaving soon, bringing sunny skies and the temperature will rise. The warmest spot on our weather map today is Miami, Florida. The temperature there is 96° under bright, sunny skies.

C. Listen: Can or Can't *Listen and circle the word you hear.*

PRONUNCIATION

can	I can swim.	I can ice skate.
can't	I can't swim.	I can't ice skate.

1. I can play tennis.
2. She can't run a mile.
3. My brother can't surf.
4. I can ice skate.
5. I can play baseball.
6. My father can sail.
7. You can't ski well.
8. I can play soccer.
9. I can't ride a bicycle.
10. My sister can roller blade.

194

Unit 14, page 125

B. Listen: A Short Vacation On Labor Day weekend, Michael and Patty took a short vacation. On Saturday they stayed in Bayside and had a terrible day. On Sunday, they stayed in Surf City and had a wonderful time. Listen to their story.

Last weekend was Labor Day. Patty and I decided to go away for a long weekend. On Saturday we drove to Bayside, to a popular beach resort. From the beginning, we had a terrible time. The weather wasn't good, it was cool and cloudy. The temperature was only 75 degrees; it was too cold to go swimming. The beach wasn't clean. There were bottles and paper in the water and on the sand because there weren't any garbage cans. And the motel, well that was my mistake. I took the room because it was cheap. But it was near a busy highway and there was a lot of noise from the trucks and cars so we couldn't sleep. The rooms were small, the bed was uncomfortable, the towels were dirty. We had a terrible time.

So, we left early Sunday morning and we drove to Surf City. What a difference! The day was sunny and hot with a temperature of 90 degrees. This time, we found a beautiful motel. It was in a quiet area, away from traffic. The rooms were large and bright. The bed was comfortable and the towels were clean and fresh. The beach was clean and white and we were in the water most of the day. We had a wonderful time. We plan to come back to Surf City next summer.

Page 125

C. Listen: a weekend vacation Listen to each sentence and circle the beach that it describes.

1. The motel was old.
2. The water was dirty.
3. The weather was sunny and hot.
4. The beach was clean.
5. The bed was uncomfortable.
6. The towels were clean and fresh.
7. The room was large.
8. The motel was in a noisy area.
9. The water was clean.
10. There was garbage in the water.

Unit 15, page 133

B. Listen: Ali's morning Listen to the tape. Where did he go first, second, third, etc.? Number the locations from 1 to 7 on the map on page 132.

I always walk downtown on Saturday morning. It's the only morning I have free all week. So, last Saturday morning I walked downtown as usual. First, I went to the bank and deposited my paycheck. I got $100 in cash. Then, I went to the shoe store because I needed a new pair of sneakers. I looked at a few pairs and I tried on two or three, but I didn't buy anything. Then I stopped at the gas company. There were a lot of people there and I waited in line fifteen minutes to pay my bill. I had to pay $20. The post office is next to the gas company, so I bought stamps and I mailed a letter to my brother. I spent ten dollars there. Well, I felt a little hungry, so I stopped at the coffee shop and ordered juice, a cup of coffee, and a donut. The bill was $2.50 and I left a 50-cent tip. After that I walked over to the library. They have a lot of newspapers and I read the Arabic language paper from my country. Also, I finally applied for a library card and took out a book on car repairs. Next, I stopped at the camera store. I picked up the pictures from my son's birthday party. I also dropped off a roll of film and bought a new roll. Altogether, I spent $17 there. That was my last stop before I walked back home.

page 134

E. Listen: Past Tense Verbs Listen and fill in the past tense verb.

1. I walked downtown.
2. I deposited my paycheck in the bank.
3. I got $100 in cash.
4. I tried on some sneakers.
5. I didn't buy anything.
6. There were a lot of people in line.
7. I waited in line fifteen minutes.
8. I mailed a letter to my brother.
9. I spent $10 at the post office.
10. I stopped at the coffee shop.
11. I ordered a cup of coffee.
12. The bill was $2.50.
13. I left a 50-cent tip.
14. I took out a book on car repairs.
15. I picked up my pictures.
16. I didn't stop at the drugstore.

page 134

A. Listen: -ed

Final -ed is pronounced as /t/ or /d/ after most verbs. Do not add a syllable to the verb.

EXAMPLE

play	played	walk	walked
mail	mailed	stop	stopped
try	tried	look	looked

Final -ed is pronounced as /Id/ after **t** and **d**. Add a syllable to the verb.

EXAMPLE

need	needed
wait	waited

Underline the verb in each sentence. Then, listen to each sentence on the tape. Write the number of syllables you hear in each verb. Read the sentences to a partner.

EXAMPLE

1. _Ali_ walked downtown.

2. _He_ needed a pair of sneakers.

1. ____ Ali walked to the bank.
2. ____ He wanted a pair of sneakers.
3. ____ Ali stopped at the gas company.
4. ____ He waited in line for 15 minutes.
5. ____ He talked to some of the people in line.
6. ____ Ali needed some stamps.
7. ____ Ali mailed a letter to his brother.
8. ____ He looked at the newspaper from his country.
9. ____ Ali picked up some pictures.
10. ____ He started home again.

Unit 16, page 147

B. Listen: Oscar Listen to Oscar talk about his life. The second time you listen, write one past tense verb under each picture. Retell his story.

Hi. My name is Oscar Vega. I'm 21 years old and I'm a student here at Dallas Community College. I was born in Mexico, in a small town in the central part. I started school there when I was six years old. Let's see, what can I remember? One summer, when I was seven, I fell off my bicycle and broke my arm. When I was in second grade, I got the chicken pox. My four brothers and my sister got the chicken pox, too. And all the time when I was a kid, I played soccer—before school, after school, and on the weekends. I made the school team. When I was twelve, our team won the local championship and I got a trophy. I still have that trophy in my room. And then, when I was 14, I moved to the United States with my parents, here, to Dallas. My aunt and uncle lived here already. I started high school. I went to Dallas High School. I really didn't like it at first, because I didn't know anyone and I wasn't on the soccer team. But I knew a little English and I learned it fast. The year I turned 16 was great for me. My father taught me how to drive and I got my driver's license. When I was 17 I found my first job at a pizza place. I know, a Mexican boy making Italian pizza. But I was good at it. After I graduated from high school, I started college. I'm still working at the pizza place, but now I'm the assistant manager. Now, I'm majoring in business and working nights and weekends.